The Great Discourse on Causation

The Translator

Bhikkhu Bodhi is a Buddhist monk of American nationality, born in New York City in 1944. After completing a doctorate in philosophy at Claremont Graduate School, he came to Sri Lanka in 1972 for the purpose of entering the Sangha. He received novice ordination in 1972 and higher ordination as a bhikkhu in 1973, both under the eminent scholar-monk, Ven. Balangoda Ananda Maitreya, with whom he studied Pali and Dhamma. He is the author of several works on Theravada Buddhism, including four translations of major Pali suttas along with their commentaries. Since 1984 he has been the Editor for the Buddhist Publication Society, and its President since 1988.

The Great Discourse on Causation

The Mahānidāna Sutta and its Commentaries

Translated from the Pali by

Bhikkhu Bodhi

Buddhist Publication Society
Kandy • Sri Lanka

Buddhist Publication Society
P.O. Box 61
54, Sangharaja Mawatha
Kandy, Sri Lanka

First published in 1984
2nd edition 1995
Reprinted 2000

National Library of Sri Lanka –
Cataloguing–in–Publication Data

Bodhi himi

The great discourse on causation : the Mahanidana Sutta and its commentaries / Bhikkhu Bodhi. – 2nd ed. – Kandy : Buddhist Publication Society, 2000

140,xiip. ; 22cm. – First published in 1984

ISBN 955–24–0117–8

i. 181.043 DDC 21 ii. Title
1. Philosophy, Buddhist 2. Buddhism

ISBN 955–24–0117–8

Typeset at the BPS

Printed in Sri Lanka by
Karunaratne & Sons Ltd.
67 U.D.A., Industrial Estate
Katuwana
Homagama

CONTENTS

TRANSLATOR'S PREFACE

The present work follows the precedent set by my previous two works for making available in English major Pali Buddhist suttas accompanied by their classical commentaries.* It offers a translation of the Mahānidāna Sutta along with abundant selections from its principal exegetical texts, elucidating it from the Theravada Buddhist perspective. The Mahānidāna Sutta itself is the fifteenth sutta in the *Dīgha Nikāya*, the first division of the Sutta Piṭaka belonging to the Pali Canon. It is the longest discourse of the Buddha dealing with dependent arising (*paṭiccasamuppāda*), a topic pointed to by the Buddha himself as the central principle of his teaching. The word *nidāna* in the title shows up frequently in a chain of synonyms signifying the idea of cause. Within the text it has been rendered as "source," the primary word "cause" being reserved for the more common *hetu*. But an intelligible rendering of the sutta's title required that I take a little freedom with the terms, so there it has been translated "causation," which certainly communicates the intended sense far more smoothly than anything that could have been derived from "source." The prefix *mahā*, meaning "great," is often added to the title of a long sutta, usually to distinguish it from a shorter sutta of the same name. But from the high regard with which the Mahānidāna Sutta is viewed within the Theravada Buddhist tradition, it seems unlikely that the compilers of the Pali Canon called it a "great discourse" merely as an indication of its length. Far more probably their intention was to emphasize the sutta's own intrinsic greatness, which they saw in the profundity of its subject matter, the thoroughness of its exposition, and the wealth of its implications for an understanding of the human condition.

The exegetical texts on the sutta consist of a commentary and a subcommentary. The former is found in the *Sumaṅgalavilāsinī*, the complete commentary (*aṭṭhakathā*) to the Dīgha Nikāya. It is the work of the great Indian expositor Bhadantācariya Buddhaghosa, who composed it on the basis of the ancient Sinhala commentaries he studied at the

---

**The Discourse on the All-Embracing Net of Views: The Brahmajāla Sutta and its Commentaries*, and *The Discourse on the Root of Existence: The Mūlapariyāya Sutta and its Commentaries*, both published by the Buddhist Publication Society, 1978 (rep. 1992) and 1980 (rep. 1992), respectively.

Mahāvihāra in Sri Lanka in the fifth century C.E. The subcommentary (*ṭīkā*), written to clarify the primary commentary and to carry further the explication of the sutta, is ascribed to Bhadantācariya Dhammapāla. He too was an Indian, a resident of Badaratittha near Madras, and probably lived in the century following Buddhaghosa. The commentary, in giving an account of dependent arising, could have been very much longer than it is, but one circumstance made a bulky work unnecessary. In his monumental treatise, the *Visuddhimagga*, Bhadantācariya Buddhaghosa had already written a full exposition of the subject, and thus, when he took up the commentary to the Mahānidāna Sutta, he did not have to repeat himself on every point but could focus his attention on the special issues raised by the sutta itself. As to the general problems posed by dependent arising, those he could deal with in a synoptical manner, sending the earnest student to the *Visuddhimagga* for details.

The format of this work is the same as that of my previous translations. The sutta is given first without comment and with only a few notes. This is followed by the commentarial section which, like those of the earlier works, has been composed selectively. My guiding principle has been to include everything of doctrinal importance, especially from the commentary, while omitting irrelevant digressions and side remarks as well as the copious grammatical and etymological clarifications inevitable in days when commentaries also functioned as Pali dictionaries. The passages selected from the two exegetical texts have been arranged according to the numerical divisions of the sutta. Thus the explanation for any sutta statement elucidated in the commentaries can be found by first looking up the corresponding passage number of the commentarial section and then locating the sutta statement itself, usually signalled by the capitalization of its key phrase. The page numbers of the PTS editions of the Dīgha Nikāya and of its commentary, the *Sumaṅgalavilāsinī*, are embedded in the text in square brackets. I did not include page references to the PTS edition of the Dīgha Nikāya Ṭīkā, as the margins of that work contain cross-references to the pages of the *Sumaṅgalavilāsinī* upon which the Ṭīkā is elaborating.

The Introduction explains the main principles of the sutta and explores some of the lines of thought stimulated by the Buddha's suggestive utterances. Though the first section of the Introduction gives a short overview of dependent arising, the essay is not intended as a primer on the doctrine but generally presupposes prior familiarity with it gained from other reliable sources. As might be expected from a discourse spoken to demonstrate the full depth of dependent arising, the Mahānidāna Sutta contains several terse and very pithy passages the meaning of which is not at all evident; yet these are not directly elaborated upon either in other suttas or in the commentaries. Therefore, to uncover their meaning, a certain amount of individual interpretation was required, with reflection and intuition contributing as much to the conclusions arrived at as study of the texts. The results of these investigations may be seen particularly in the sections on contact, the "hidden vortex," the "pathways for designations," and in the expansion of the Buddha's very concise arguments against the three "considerations of self."

One prominent feature of the exegetical texts on the Mahānidāna Sutta called for special explanation on its own. This is their treatment of dependent arising according to the Abhidhamma system of conditional relations. If I had attempted to deal with this in the Introduction I would have had to digress too far from the main thread of the discussion and would have placed too great a burden on the essay. To avoid this I have added an appendix in which I devote to this method of treatment the separate attention it requires.

Though each reader will find his or her own way of approaching the material presented here, intensive study will probably be most fruitful if the sutta is read first by itself, a second time in conjunction with the introductory essay, and a third time in conjunction with the commentarial exegesis.

BHIKKHU BODHI

TEXTS USED

I. Primary Sources

Dīgha Nikāya: Mahāvagga Pāli. Burmese Buddhasāsana Council edition; Rangoon, 1954.

The Dīgha Nikāya. Edited by T.W. Rhys Davids and J. Estlin Carpenter. Volume II. London: Pali Text Society, 1903.

Dīgha Nikāya Aṭṭhakathā (Sumaṅgalavilāsinī): Mahāvagga Aṭṭhakathā. Burmese Buddhasāsana Council edition; Rangoon, 1957.

Dīgha Nikāya Ṭīkā: Mahāvagga Ṭīkā. Burmese Buddhasāsana Council edition; Rangoon, 1961.

Dīghanikāyaṭṭhakathāṭīkā Līnatthavaṇṇanā. Edited by Lily De Silva. Volumes I and II. London: Luzac and Company, Ltd. for the Pali Text Society, 1970.

II. Previous Translations Consulted

Ñāṇamoli Thera. "The Mahānidāna Suttanta." Unpublished manuscript translation.

Rhys Davids, T.W. and C.A.F., trans. *Dialogues of the Buddha*, 5th ed., Part II. London: Luzac and Company, Ltd. for the Pali Text Society, 1966.

III. Other Related Works

Bodhi, Bhikkhu, ed. *A Comprehensive Manual of Abhidhamma.* Kandy: BPS, 1993.

Bodhi, Bhikkhu, trans. *The Discourse on the All-Embracing Net of Views: The Brahmajāla Sutta and its Commentaries.* Kandy: BPS, 1978.

Ñāṇamoli, Bhikkhu, trans. *The Path of Purification* (*Visuddhimagga*) *by Bhadantācariya Buddhaghosa*, 4th ed. Kandy: BPS, 1979. Especially Chapter XVII.

Nyanatiloka. *Buddhist Dictionary*, 4th rev. ed. Kandy: BPS, 1980 (entries "Paccaya" and "Paṭiccasamuppāda").

Nyanatiloka. *A Guide through the Abhidhamma Piṭaka*, 3rd ed. Kandy: BPS, 1971. Appendix.

Nyanatiloka. *The Significance of Dependent Origination*. (Wheel No. 140), Kandy: BPS, 1969.

Piyadassi Thera. *Dependent Origination*: *Paṭicca Samuppāda*. (Wheel No. 15a/b), Kandy: BPS, 1959.

Warder, A.K. *Indian Buddhism*. Delhi: Motilal Banarsidass, 1970. Chapter 5.

LIST OF ABBREVIATIONS

A.	Aṅguttara Nikāya
Cy.	Dīgha Nikāya Aṭṭhakathā (Commentary)
D.	Dīgha Nikāya
Dhs.	Dhammasaṅgaṇī
Dhs.A.	Dhammasaṅgaṇī Aṭṭhakathā (Aṭṭhasālinī)
M.	Majjhima Nikāya
M. Nd.	Mahā Niddesa
Pṭs.	Paṭisambhidāmagga
Pug.	Puggalapaññatti
S.	Saṁyutta Nikāya
Sn.	Sutta Nipāta
Sub. Cy.	Dīgha Nikāya Ṭīkā (Subcommentary)
Vin.	Vinaya Piṭaka
Vism.	Visuddhimagga

References to Vism. are followed by the chapter and section number of Bhikkhu Ñāṇamoli's translation, *The Path of Purification* (see Texts Used). Otherwise, all references are to Pali Text Society editions.

INTRODUCTION

Dependent Arising

In the Theravada Buddhist tradition the Mahānidāna Sutta is regarded as one of the profoundest discourses spoken by the Buddha. Its principal theme is *paṭiccasamuppāda*, "dependent arising," and that immediately alerts us to its importance. For the Pali Canon makes it quite plain that dependent arising is not merely one strand of doctrine among others, but the radical insight at the heart of the Buddha's teaching, the insight from which everything else unfolds. For the Buddha himself, during his period of struggle for enlightenment, dependent arising came as the astonishing, eye-opening discovery that ended his groping in the dark: " 'Arising, arising'—thus, bhikkhus, in regard to things unheard before, there arose in me vision, knowledge, wisdom, understanding, and light" (S.XII,65; ii,105). A series of suttas shows the same discovery to be the essence of each Buddha's attainment of enlightenment (S.XIII,4-10). Once enlightened, the mission of a Tathāgata, a Perfect One, is to proclaim dependent arising to the world (S.XII,20; ii, 25-26). So often does the Buddha do this, in discourse after discourse, that dependent arising soon becomes regarded as the quintessence of his teaching. When the arahat Assaji was asked to state the Master's message as concisely as possible, he said it was the doctrine that phenomena arise and cease through causes (Vin.i,40). With a single sentence the Buddha dispels all doubt about the correctness of this summary: "He who sees dependent arising sees the Dhamma, he who sees the Dhamma sees dependent arising" (M.28; i,191).

The reason dependent arising is assigned so much weight lies in two essential contributions it makes to the teaching. First, it provides the teaching with its primary ontological principle, its key for understanding the nature of being. Second, it provides the framework that guides its programme for deliverance, a causal account of the origination and cessation of suffering. These two contributions, though separable in thought, come together in the thesis that makes the Buddha's teaching a "doctrine of awakening": that suffering ultimately arises due to ignorance about the nature of being and ceases through wisdom, direct understanding of the nature of being.

The ontological principle contributed by dependent arising is, as its name suggests, the arising of phenomena in dependence on conditions. At a stroke this principle disposes of the notion of static self-contained entities and shows that the "texture" of being is through and through relational. Whatever comes into being originates through conditions, stands with the support of conditions, and ceases when its conditions cease. But dependent arising teaches something more rigorous than a simple assertion of general conditionality. What it teaches is *specific conditionality* (*idappaccayatā*), the arising of phenomena in dependence on specific conditions. This is an important point often overlooked in standard accounts of the doctrine. Specific conditionality correlates phenomena in so far as they belong to *types*. It holds that phenomena of a given type originate only through the conditions appropriate to that type, never in the absence of those conditions, never through the conditions appropriate to some other type. Thus dependent arising, as a teaching of specific conditionality, deals primarily with structures. It treats phenomena, not in terms of their isolated connections, but in terms of their patterns—recurrent patterns that exhibit the invariableness of law:

> Bhikkhus, what is dependent arising? "With birth as condition aging and death come to be"—whether Tathāgatas arise or not, that element stands, that structuredness of phenomena, that fixed determination of phenomena, specific conditionality. That a Tathāgata awakens to and comprehends. Having awakened to it and comprehended it, he explains it, teaches it, proclaims it, establishes it, reveals it, analyzes it, and clarifies it, saying: "See, bhikkhus, with birth as condition aging and death come to be." The reality in that, the undelusiveness, invariability, specific conditionality—this, bhikkhus, is called dependent arising. (S.XII,20; ii,25-6)

The basic formula for dependent arising appears in the suttas countless times: "When there is this, that comes to be; with the arising of this, that arises. When this is absent, that does not come to be; with the cessation of this, that ceases."[1] This gives the principle in the abstract, stripped of any reference to a content. But the Buddha is not interested in abstract formulas devoid of content; for him content is all-important. His teaching is concerned with a problem—the problem of suffering (*dukkha*)—and with the task of bringing suffering to an end. Dependent arising is introduced because it is relevant to these concerns, indeed not merely relevant but indispensable. It defines the framework needed to understand the problem and also indicates the approach that must be taken if that problem is to be resolved.

The suffering with which the Buddha's teaching is concerned has a far deeper meaning than personal unhappiness, discontent, or psychological stress. It includes these, but it goes beyond. The problem in its fullest measure is existential suffering, the suffering of bondage to the round of repeated birth and death. The round, the Buddha teaches, has been turning without beginning, and as long as it turns it inevitably brings "aging and death, sorrow, lamentation, pain, grief, and despair." To gain deliverance from suffering, therefore, requires more than relief from its transient individual manifestations. It requires nothing short of total liberation from the round.

In order to end the round, the conditions that sustain it have to be eliminated; and to eliminate them it is necessary to know what they are, how they hold together, and what must be done to extinguish their causal force. Though the round has no first point, no cause outside itself, it does have a distinct generative structure, a set of conditions internal to itself which keeps it in motion. The teaching of dependent arising discloses this set of conditions. It lays them out in an interlocking sequence which makes it clear how existence repeatedly renews itself from within and how it will continue into the future through the continued activation of these causes. Most importantly, however, dependent arising shows that the round can be stopped. It traces the sequence of conditions to its most fundamental factors. Then it points out that these can be eliminated and that with their elimination the round of rebirths and its attendant suffering are brought to a halt.

As an account of the causal structure of the round, dependent arising appears in the suttas in diverse formulations. The fullest and most common contains twelve factors. The formula has two sides. One shows the sequence of origination, the other the sequence of cessation:

> Bhikkhus, what is dependent arising? With ignorance as condition volitional formations come to be; with volitional formations as condition, consciousness; with consciousness as condition, mentality-materiality; with mentality-materiality as condition, the six sense bases; with the six sense bases as condition, contact; with contact as condition, feeling; with feeling as condition, craving; with craving as condition, clinging; with clinging as condition, existence; with existence as condition, birth; with birth as condition, aging and death, sorrow, lamentation, pain, grief, and despair come to

Due to ignorance, formally defined as the non-knowledge of 4 N. Truths

be. Such is the origin of this entire mass of suffering. This, bhikkhus, is called dependent arising.

But with the remainderless fading away and cessation of ignorance volitional formations cease; with the cessation of volitional formations consciousness ceases; with the cessation of consciousness mentality-materiality ceases; with the cessation of mentality-materiality the six sense bases cease; with the cessation of the six sense bases contact ceases; with the cessation of contact feeling ceases; with the cessation of feeling craving ceases; with the cessation of craving clinging ceases; with the cessation of clinging existence ceases; with the cessation of existence birth ceases; with the cessation of birth, aging and death, sorrow, lamentation, pain, grief, and despair cease. Such is the cessation of this entire mass of suffering. (S.XII,1; ii,1-2)[2]

The prevailing interpretation regards the series as spanning three successive lives, the twelve factors representing the causal and resultant phases of these lives alternated to show the round's inherent capacity for self-regeneration. Thus ignorance and volitional formations represent the causal phase of the previous life which brought about existence in the present; the five factors from consciousness through feeling are their fruit, the resultant phase of the present life. Craving, clinging, and existence represent renewed causal activity in the present life; birth and aging and death sum up the resultant phase of the future life.

At the risk of oversimplification the sequence can be briefly explained as follows. Due to ignorance—formally defined as non-knowledge of the Four Noble Truths—a person engages in ethically motivated action, which may be wholesome or unwholesome, bodily, verbal, or mental. These actions, referred to here as volitional formations, constitute kamma. At the time of rebirth kamma conditions the re-arising of consciousness, which comes into being bringing along its psychophysical adjuncts, "mentality-materiality" (*nāma-rūpa*). In dependence on the psychophysical adjuncts, the six sense bases develop—the five outer senses and the mind-base. Through these, contact takes place between consciousness and its objects, and contact in turn conditions feeling. In response to feeling craving springs up, and if it grows firm, leads into clinging. Driven by clinging actions are performed with the potency to generate new existence. These actions, kamma backed by craving, eventually bring a new existence: birth followed by aging and death.

To prevent misunderstanding it has to be stressed that the distribution of the twelve factors into three lives is an expository device em-

One's actions AKA VF constitute kamma. At time of rebirth kamma conditions the re-arising of conscience which comes into being bringing along

its physcophysical adjuncts * P4

ployed for the purpose of exhibiting the inner dynamics of the round. It should not be read as implying hard and fast divisions, for in lived experience the factors are always intertwined. The past causes include craving, clinging, and existence, the present ones ignorance and volitional formations; the present resultants begin with birth and end in death, and future birth and death will be incurred by the same resultants. Moreover, the present resultant and causal phases should not be seen as temporally segregated from each other, as if assigned to different periods of life. Rather, through the entire course of life, they succeed one another with incredible rapidity in an alternating sequence of result and response. A past kamma ripens in present results; these trigger off new action; the action is followed by more results; and these are again followed by still more action. So it has gone on through time without beginning, and so it continues.

From this it is clear that dependent arising does not describe a set of causes somehow underlying experience, mysteriously hidden out of view. What it describes is the fundamental pattern of experience as such when enveloped by ignorance as to the basic truths about itself. This pattern is always present, always potentially accessible to our awareness, only without the guidance of the Buddha's teaching it will not be properly attended to, and thus will not be seen for what it is. It takes a Buddha to point out the startling truth that the basic pattern of experience is itself the source of our bondage, "the origin of this entire mass of suffering."

Cast and Setting

Among the many suttas on dependent arising spoken by the Buddha, the Mahānidāna Sutta is the longest and the most detailed; it is also perhaps the richest as a source of insights. Despite its length, however, the Mahānidāna Sutta does not give the most complete formal exposition of dependent arising. It lacks the abstract formula and a statement of the sequence of cessation. Moreover, its series of conditions omits three factors of the standard version: ignorance, volitional formations, and the six sense bases (*avijjā, saṅkhārā, saḷāyatana*). These omissions have led some scholars to suggest that the twelvefold formulation may be a later augmentation of a shorter original; but such suggestions remain purely conjectural, misleading, and objectionable on doctrinal and textual grounds. All in all, the omissions of the Mahānidāna Sutta are more than compensated for by its detailed explanations, interesting digressions, and supplementary sections. Indeed, it might well

Dependent arising does not describble a set of causes somehow underlying experience, mysteriously hidden out of view. What it describes is the fundamental pattern of experience as such when enveloped by ignorance be suspected, contrary to the thesis of historical development, that in the present sutta the Buddha has varied the usual exposition expressly to create an opportunity for such special methods of treatment.[3]

The sutta begins when the Venerable Ānanda, the Buddha's personal attendant, approaches the Master and exclaims that though dependent arising is deep and appears deep, to himself it seems "as clear as clear can be" (*uttānakuttānaka*). The Pali word *uttāna*, "clear," also means "shallow," and is sometimes contrasted with "deep" (*gambhīra*), as in the example given in the commentary. Thus Ānanda's words, though doubtlessly innocent and respectful in intent, confront the Buddha with a challenge. They call upon him to reconfirm the profundity of his teaching by demonstrating the depth of its most distinctive doctrine.

The Buddha first checks the Venerable Ānanda with the gentle admonition: "Do not say so, Ānanda! Do not say so, Ānanda!" These words, according to the commentary, intimate both praise and reproach. They praise Ānanda by implying his special qualities which enabled him to comprehend dependent arising so clearly: his accumulation of merit over many lives, his previous study, his attainment of stream-entry, his vast erudition. They reproach him by hinting at the limitations of his understanding: he could never have penetrated conditionality without the guidance of the Buddha; he still remains a stream-enterer barely past the entrance to the path; even when he reaches the final stage of arahatship he will not attain the knowledge of a chief disciple, a paccekabuddha, or a fully enlightened Buddha. In the sutta itself, after restraining the Venerable Ānanda, the Buddha corrects him by repeating his original statement on the profundity of dependent arising: "This dependent arising, Ānanda, is deep and it appears deep." The phrase about the deep appearance, the subcommentary says, is added to stress the fact that dependent arising is exclusively deep. We might perhaps understand the first phrase to refer to dependent arising as an objective principle, the second to refer to the verbal exposition of that principle. Together they indicate that dependent arising is deep both in essence and in manifestation.

The commentary takes up the Buddha's statement and amplifies it by explaining four respects in which dependent arising can be called deep: because of its depth of meaning, depth of phenomena, depth of teaching, and depth of penetration. As this fourfold analysis is found in several places in the commentaries, it merits some consideration. The first two kinds of depth apply in opposite ways to the link between each pair of factors. The "depth of meaning" (*atthagambhīratā*) applies to the link viewed from the standpoint of the effect looking back to its condition, the "depth of phenomena" (*dhammagambhīratā*) from the standpoint of the condition looking forward to its effect.[4] Each standpoint highlights a different kind of profundity. In the former case the profundity lies in the invariable dependence of the effect on its condition: how the effect always comes into being and continues with the support of its condition, never in the absence of the condition. In the latter case the profundity consists in the efficacy of the condition: how it exercises its causative role in relation to its effect.

The "depth of teaching" (*desanāgambhīratā*) refers to the diversity in methods used by the Buddha to expound dependent arising. The diversity is dictated by two considerations: first, by the complexity of the subject itself, which only reveals its multiple facets when illuminated from various angles; and second, by the persons being taught, who can only understand the teaching when its presentation is adapted to their needs and capacities. As the Buddha excels in both "eloquent exposition" and "skillful means," the result is the great variety in his methods of teaching the doctrine.

The fourth kind of depth, "depth of penetration" (*paṭivedhagambhīratā*), derives its meaning from the exegetical term *sabhāva*, "intrinsic nature," used in the commentaries to define the notion of *dhammā*, "phenomena." Etymologically, the word *dhamma* means "that which supports": according to the commentarial gloss of the word, what *dhammā* support is their own intrinsic nature.[5] At the ontological level a *dhamma* and its intrinsic nature coincide: there is no fundamental difference in mode of being between a thing and its nature. But epistemological purposes allow a distinction to be drawn between them. The *dhamma* then becomes the phenomenon in its concreteness, the intrinsic nature the set of qualities it actualizes. The intrinsic nature includes both the "particular characteristic" (*visesalakkhaṇa*), i.e. the qualities determining the *dhamma* as a thing of a particular sort—as earth element, as feeling, as volition, etc.—and the "general characteristics" (*sāmaññalakkhaṇa*), the features it shares with other things, especially the triad of impermanence, suffering, and non-self. It is through the characteristics that the intrinsic nature of the dhamma is penetrated during the development of insight (*vipassanā*). Therefore, for each factor of dependent arising, the commentary enumerates the principal characteristics, which the subcommentary takes up for elucidation.

Shortly after his enlightenment, while still pondering whether or not to teach the Dhamma to others, the Buddha had realized that "a generation delighting in attachment" would meet difficulty in understanding dependent arising (M.26; i,167). Now, with the closing sentence of the introductory section, he states the consequence of not understanding it. Because it has not understood and penetrated "this Dhamma" of dependent arising, "this generation"—the world of living beings—has become entangled in defilements and wrong views and thus cannot escape from saṁsāra, the round of rebirths, "with its plane of misery, unfortunate destinations, and lower realms." The statement confirms the depth of dependent arising even without need for further argument or discussion. The whole world of living beings revolves in the round of birth and death, repeatedly returning to the lower worlds, because of its failure to comprehend this one principle. The penetration of dependent arising therefore becomes a matter of the utmost urgency. It is the gateway to liberation through which all must pass who seek deliverance from the round.

Specific Conditionality

The rest of the sutta, according to the commentary, develops from the Buddha's two pronouncements of §1: "this dependent arising is deep," and "this generation has become like a tangled skein." The former leads into the first main division of the sutta, the detailed account of dependent arising (§§2-22); the latter is followed up in the second main division, in which the Buddha undertakes a methodical investigation of views of self (§§23-32). All these sections are technically classified as "exposition of the round" (*vaṭṭakathā*); they illustrate the noble truths of suffering and its origin. But the Buddha also teaches the ending of the round (*vivaṭṭakathā*), the noble truths of the cessation of suffering and the path. These truths are shown elliptically in the third and final division of the sutta (§§33-35). They are represented by the arahat, the liberated one, who has disentangled the chain of conditions and passed beyond the confines of the round.

The Buddha begins his instruction proper with a short catechism on dependent arising intended to elicit the condition for each dependent factor in the series (§2). The catechism pursues the series in reverse order from aging and death being dependent on birth back to consciousness being dependent on mentality-materiality. He then states the entire sequence again in forward order, without the catechism, adding the regular refrain identifying the series as the origin of suffering (§3). This completes the brief account, conspicuous by the absence of three familiar factors—ignorance, volitional formations, and the six sense bases. There then follows a longer exposition in which the Buddha returns to each proposition of the original sequence and elaborates upon its meaning. His explanation serves three main purposes: (i) to elucidate the meaning of specific conditionality by showing what is involved when one phenomenon is called a specific condition for another; (ii) to facilitate a more precise understanding of dependent arising by analyzing the conditioning factors into their constituents; and (iii) to demonstrate how each condition contributes to the arising of the state dependent on it.

In the sutta the Buddha does not offer a formal definition of specific conditionality; even the abstract formula is not mentioned. But the explanation of the connection between each pair of factors suffices to make the underlying principle clear. Specific conditionality is a relationship of indispensability and dependency: the indispensability of the condition (e.g. birth) to the arisen state (e.g. aging and death), the dependency of the arisen state upon its condition. The sutta's explanation accentuates the minimal requirement for one phenomenon to be the condition for another. It shows conditionality determined negatively, as the impossibility of the dependent state appearing in the absence of its condition. Other suttas characterize conditionality in more positive terms, as a contributory influence passing from the condition to the dependent state. This much is already implied by the second phrase of the abstract formula: "With the arising of this, that arises." Elsewhere more is added. The condition originates (*samudaya*) the dependent state, provides it with a source (*nidāna*), generates it (*jātika*), gives it being (*pabhava*), nourishes it (*āhāra*), acts as its foundation (*upanisā*), causes it to surge (*upayāpeti*).[6] The commentaries, too, show their sensitivity to this twofold meaning of conditionality when they first define a condition as a state indispensable to another state's arising or presence, then add: "a condition has the characteristic of assisting, for any given state that assists the presence or arising of a given state is called the latter's condition" (Vism. XVII,68).

When dependent arising is explained in terms of indispensability, this cautions us against interpreting it as a principle of causal necessitation. Though the condition may play an active causal role in arousing the dependent state, it does not necessitate the latter. In certain cases an inseparable bond connects the two, so that whenever one arises the other is bound to follow, e.g. birth is always followed by death. But there are other cases where such a bond is lacking, where the condition may occur without arousing the dependent state. As abstruse as this point may seem, it has the profoundest implications for a teaching of deliverance. For if dependent arising described a series in which each factor necessitated the next, the series could never be broken. All human effort directed to liberation would be futile and the round would have to turn forever. But a relationship of conditionality, unlike a necessitarian one, allows for a margin of freedom in responding to the condition.

The place in the sequence of conditions where that margin takes on the greatest importance is the link between feeling and craving. It is at that brief moment when the present resultant phase has come to a culmination in feeling, but the present causal phase has not yet begun, that the issue of bondage and liberation is decided. If the response to feeling is governed by ignorance and craving, the round continues to revolve; if the response replaces craving with restraint, mindfulness, and methodical attention, a movement is made in the direction of cessation.

Though the formula for dependent arising presents the factors in a linear sequence, this should not be taken to imply that they fit together in a temporally progressive chain of causes and effects. As was pointed out earlier, the selection of factors and their sequential arrangement are made from the instructional point of view, the purpose being to expose the inner dynamics of the round in order to demonstrate how to dismantle it. By resorting to abstraction, each phrase in the formula treats as a one-to-one bond what is in actuality a situation of immense complexity involving a multitude of conditions arousing and sustaining a multitude of dependent phenomena. In some cases a strong causal influence operates from one factor to another, in others the relation is one of mere necessary dependence. In some cases the formula describes a movement from condition to effect occupying time, even a succession of lives; in others it portrays a cross-section of events occurring at the same moment.

To clarify the relationship between each conditioning factor and its dependent state, the exegetical texts apply the system of twenty-four conditional relations set forth in the *Paṭṭhāna*, the seventh and last book of the Abhidhamma Piṭaka. The commentary does so summarily, generally mentioning only the major headings of conascence condition and decisive support condition; in more complicated cases it simply says that one is a condition for the other "in many ways." The subcommentary expands the summary, enumerating the types of conditions subsumed under the major headings and spelling out the "many ways." In the Appendix the twenty-four conditions have been briefly sketched and exemplified in their application to dependent arising. Thus here only the two main conditions will be discussed.

The conascence condition (*sahajāta-paccaya*) and decisive support condition (*upanissaya-paccaya*) are the primary examples of two contrasting kinds of conditional relationship, distinguished by their temporal mode. *Conascence* is the prototype of the tie between simultaneous phenomena, things sharing a common origination and cessation. It includes under itself such other conditions of the *Paṭṭhāna* system as mutuality, support, association, and presence; some of these are narrower in scope (e.g. mutuality), others broader (e.g. presence). *Decisive support* is the most prominent condition relating non-simultaneous phenomena. It signifies the powerful causal influence one thing may exert on another when they are separated by an interval of time—either a moment's lapse (object decisive support), immediate succession (proximity decisive support), or an extended period (natural decisive support). There are other conditional relations which do not fall neatly under these two headings, but these two suffice to show the diversity possible in the interrelations of the factors of dependent arising. Such diversity precludes attempts to force these relations into a uniform mould either of simultaneity or succession, errors occasionally committed by earlier interpreters of the doctrine.

The Sequence of Conditions

In the Mahānidāna Sutta the Buddha expounds the sequence of conditions in reverse order. Conceptually there may be no difference in meaning whether the sequence is presented in forward order or in reverse. But the Buddha's exposition of the Dhamma has another purpose besides the bare communication of conceptual meaning. That purpose is to lead on: to arouse the will and set it moving towards the intended goal of the teaching, the cessation of suffering. The reverse order presentation of the sequence serves that purpose with an effectiveness unmatched by the other. The forward order presentation expounds dependent arising from the standpoint of completed comprehension: it is the Buddha revealing to others what he has himself fully fathomed from the bottom up. The reverse order presentation expounds the series from the standpoint of existential inquiry. It at once confronts the auditor with the problem of his being, then takes him on a step-by-step descent down the chain of conditions that underlies that problem. In so doing it recapitulates the process by which the Buddha himself discovered dependent arising, and thus tends to kindle a spark of the same enlightenment.[7]

The series begins with aging and death (*jarā-maraṇa*) as the epitome of the suffering inherent in sentient existence. This is the spur which awakens a sense of urgency and sets off the search for a solution. The statement that aging and death occur with birth (*jāti*) as condition (§4) drives home the point that suffering is ineluctable. Merely to have come into being, to have taken up a body, is to be thrown irresistibly towards decline, decay, and death by nothing else than the passage of time itself. But the statement has another side: it points in the direction of a solution. Whatever suffering there is, all that is conditioned; it occurs in dependence on birth. If birth also is dependent on some condition, and that condition can be removed, then it would be possible to end all suffering. Birth is the first point in each individual existence, the moment of conception. But conception, the Buddha teaches, does not occur through biological causes alone; it also involves a stream of consciousness passing over from a previous life. Thus the inquiry into the specific condition for birth takes us back beyond the moment of conception into the life which preceded it.

The condition for birth, the Buddha says, is existence (*bhava*, §5). This he analyzes as threefold: sense-sphere existence (*kāmabhava*), fine-material existence (*rūpabhava*), and immaterial existence (*arūpabhava*). Ordinarily these terms denote the realms of existence, the three tiers of saṁsāra into which rebirth can take place. But because rebirth into each realm is brought about by a particular kind of kamma, the word "existence," according to the commentaries, comes to be transferred from the realm proper to the kamma conducing to rebirth into that realm. The two are distinguished as kamma-existence (*kammabhava*) and rebirth-existence (*uppattibhava*).[8] Since rebirth-existence includes birth, the exegetical tradition interprets the existence that conditions birth as kamma-existence—the kamma of the previous life that generates the succeeding birth and sustains the vital forces throughout the entire span of life. Thus "sense-sphere existence" is the kamma leading to the sense-sphere realm, i.e. all unwholesome kamma and wholesome kamma short of the meditative attainments; "fine-material existence" is kamma leading to the fine-material realm, i.e. the four jhānas; "immaterial existence" is the kamma leading to the immaterial realm, i.e. the four immaterial attainments. As the kamma producing new existence obviously requires time before it can engender its results, existence is a condition for birth as a decisive support condition, not as a conascence condition.

The specific condition for existence in both aspects is clinging (*upādāna*): clinging to sense pleasures (*kām'upādāna*), clinging to views (*diṭṭh'upādāna*), clinging to precepts and observances (*sīlabbat'upādāna*), clinging to a doctrine of self (*attavād'upādāna*) (§6). The first is an intensification of sensual craving, the other three adherences to wrong views. In all its forms clinging has the sense of firm grasping (*daḷhagahaṇa*). This grasping induces motivated action and thus conditions kamma-existence. It also sustains the rebirth process whereby the accumulated kamma fructifies and thus it becomes a condition for rebirth-existence.[9]

The specific condition for clinging is craving (*taṇhā*). In the sutta craving has been subdivided in two ways: first, by way of its immediate object, into craving for each of the six sense objects (§7); second, by way of its projected aim, into craving for sense pleasures (*kāmataṇhā*), craving for existence (*bhavataṇhā*), and craving for non-existence (*vibhavataṇhā*) (§18). Sensual craving and clinging to sense pleasures signify the same mental factor, greed or lust (*lobha*), at different stages of intensity. The former is the initial desire for sense enjoyment, the latter the attachment which sets in through the repeated indulgence of the desire. Craving also gives rise to the clinging to views, generally to the view that favours its dominant urge. Thus craving for existence leads to a belief in the immortality of the soul, craving for non-existence to a theory of personal annihilation at death. Craving for sense pleasures can give rise either to an annihilationist view justifying full indulgence here and now, or to an eternalist view promising a heaven of delights to those with the prudence to exercise present restraint.[10]

Craving can become a condition for clinging to sense pleasures only as a decisive support, since by their definitions a time lapse must separate the two. But it can condition the other three kinds of clinging under both headings. It is a decisive support when earlier craving leads to the subsequent adoption of a wrong view, a conascence condition when craving co-exists with the view being adhered to through its influence.

Craving, in turn, comes into being with feeling as condition. Feeling (*vedanā*) is the affective tone of experience—pleasure, pain, or neutral feeling—which occurs on every occasion of experience through any of the six sense faculties. Craving can arise in response to all three kinds of feeling: as the yearning for pleasant feeling, the wish to flee from painful feeling, or the relishing of the dull peace of neutral feeling. But its strong support is pleasant feeling. For craving "seeks enjoyment here and there," and the enjoyment it seeks it finds in pleasant feeling. Pleasant feeling therefore becomes the "bait of the round" (*vaṭṭāmisa*) which maintains the insatiable drive for enjoyment.

In the usual sequence, immediately after eliciting feeling as the condition for craving, the Buddha brings in contact as the condition for feeling. Here, however, he introduces a variation. From feeling he returns to craving and then extracts from craving a new series of nine factors, each arising in dependence on its predecessor (§9). Craving leads to the *pursuit* of the objects desired, and through pursuit they are eventually gained. When *gained* one makes decisions about them: what is mine and what is yours, what is valuable and what disposable, how much I will keep and how much I will enjoy. Because of these *decisions*, thoughts of *desire and lust* arise. One develops *attachment* to the objects, adopts a *possessive* attitude towards them, and falls into *stinginess*, refusing to share things with others. Regarding everyone else with fear and suspicion, one seeks to *safeguard* one's belongings. When such greed and fear become widespread, they need only a slight provocation to explode into the violence, conflicts, and immorality spoken of in the sutta as "various evil, unwholesome phenomena."

This summary makes the purpose of the digression clear: it is to show that the principle of dependent arising can be used to understand the origins of social disorder just as effectively as it can be used to understand the origins of individual suffering. Like all other problems, the ailments of society arise from causes, and these can be traced in a sequence leading from the manifestations to the underlying roots. The conclusion drawn from this inquiry is highly significant: the causes of social disharmony lie in the human mind and all stem ultimately from craving.[11] Thus craving turns out to be the origin of suffering in more ways than one. It brings about not only continued rebirth in saṁsāra with its personal pain and sorrow, but also the cupidity, selfishness, violence, and immorality that wreck all attempts to establish peace, cooperation, and social stability. The commentary labels the two sides of craving as "craving which is the root of the round" (*vaṭṭamūlabhūtā taṇhā*) and "obsessional craving" (*samudācāra-taṇhā*). But it should be noted that the two expressions do not denote distinct types of craving; they simply point out different angles from which any given instance of craving can be viewed. For the craving that results in disorder and violence at the same time generates unwholesome kamma and maintains the round, while the craving for pleasure and existence that maintains the round also leads to the breakdown of social harmony.

Whether craving be viewed as a "root of the round" or as an obsession leading to greed and violence, it finds its condition in feeling. Thus the Buddha says, referring to these two aspects of craving: "These two phenomena, being a duality, converge into a unity in feeling." Feeling, in turn, originates from contact (*phassa*). Contact is the "coming together" (*saṅgati*) of consciousness with an object through a sense faculty. The six sense faculties—eye, ear, nose, tongue, body, and mind—are the internal bases for contact; the corresponding six sense objects are the external bases. Contact is distinguished as sixfold by way of the internal bases (§19). Simultaneously with its arising, feeling also springs up, conditioned by contact under the heading of conascence.

The next section of the discourse (§20) introduces another variation. In the standard exposition of dependent arising the sequence moves from contact to the six sense bases. In the Mahānidāna Sutta, however, the Buddha bypasses the six sense bases entirely and goes back a step to bring in mentality-materiality as the condition for contact. To dispel the perplexity this unfamiliar move might provoke, he then introduces a striking passage, not found elsewhere in the Canon, giving a methodical demonstration of his statement. As the passage employs several technical terms not defined either here or in other suttas, interpretation cannot be settled by scholarship alone but also requires reflection and intuition. Before turning to the new terms, however, it is best to review more familiar territory.

"Mentality-materiality" (*nāma-rūpa*) is a compound term usually used in the suttas to signify the psychophysical organism exclusive of consciousness, which serves as its condition. The suttas define the term analytically as follows:

> What, bhikkhus, is mentality-materiality? Feeling, perception, volition, contact, attention—this is called mentality. The four primary elements and the material form derived from them—this is called materiality. Thus this mentality and this materiality are called mentality-materiality. (S.XII,2; ii,3-4)

When mentality-materiality is correlated with the five aggregates, materiality is identified with the aggregate of material form (*rūpa*), mentality with the three aggregates of feeling (*vedanā*), perception (*saññā*), and mental formations (*saṅkhārā*).[12] Occasionally in the suttas the range of the term is extended to include the external sense bases as well: "This body and external mentality-materiality, these are a duality. Dependent on this duality there is contact" (S.XII, 19; ii,24). In such cases mentality-materiality becomes the entire experiential situation available to consciousness, the sentient organism together with its objective spheres.

"Designation-contact" (*adhivacanasamphassa*) and "impingement-contact" (*paṭighasamphassa*) are two terms peculiar to the present sutta. The commentary identifies the former with mind-contact, the latter with the five kinds of sense contact, but it does not explore the special meanings attached to these terms. The significance emerges from the Buddha's argument demonstrating how mentality-materiality is the condition for contact. The Buddha says that designation-contact is impossible in the material body (*rūpakāya*) when those qualities distinctive of the mental body (*nāmakāya*) are absent, and impingement-contact is impossible in the mental body when those qualities distinctive of the material body are absent. Thus each kind of contact, in the way stipulated, depends upon both the mental body and the material body. As mentality and materiality are here described as bodies, it is clear that they are intended in the narrower sense, as two sides of the sentient organism, rather than in the broader sense as including the objective sphere.

The argument points to the special role of contact as the meeting ground of mind and the world. Though all experience involves the union of mind and the world, of consciousness and its objects, contact represents this union most eminently. By its very definition it requires an external base (the object), an internal base (the sense faculty), and consciousness (which, from its own perspective, is always internal to itself). But experience is a two-way street, and the union represented by contact can result from movement in either direction: from the mind outwards towards the world or from the world inwards towards the mind. Outward movement occurs on occasions of mind-consciousness, when conceptual and volitional activity prevail; inward movement occurs on occasions of sense consciousness, when the mind's relation to the objects is one of passive receptivity.[13]

Outward movement begins with designation, the act of naming. By ascribing names the mind organizes the raw data of experience into a coherent picture of the world. It fits things into its conceptual schemes, evaluates them, and subordinates them to its aims. But designation cannot take place in a material body devoid of mentality. It requires the mental body to concoct and ascribe the labels, and each of the mental factors contributes its share. Even slight shades of difference between them show up in the chosen designation. Thus a difference in feeling may decide whether a person is called "friend" or "foe," a difference in perception whether a fruit is considered "ripe" or "unripe," a difference in volition whether a plank of wood is designated "future door" or "future tabletop," a difference in attention whether a distant object is designated "moving" or "stationary." When the designation is ascribed to the object, a union takes place of the designating consciousness with the designated object via the designation. That union is called "designation-contact." As the discourse unfolds, we will see that the process of designation acquires an increasingly more prominent role.

Designation-contact, as applied to external objects, presupposes sense perception to bring those objects into range of the designating consciousness. Sense perception begins with "impingement" (*paṭigha*), a technical term signifying the impact of an object on a sense faculty. When this impact is strong enough, a sense consciousness arises based on the appropriate sense faculty. The union that takes place when consciousness encounters the impingent object is termed "impingement-contact." Though properly belonging to mentality, impingement-contact cannot occur in the mental body alone. By definition it is contact occurring through the physical sense faculties, and thus it requires the material body to provide the internal bases for its arising.

The two terms, impingement and designation, have a fundamental importance which ties them to dependent arising as a whole. They again indicate the basic oscillatory pattern of experience referred to earlier, its movement back and forth between the phases of reception and response. The receptive phase sees the maturation of the kammic inflow from the past; it is represented here by impingement issuing in sense consciousness. The responsive phase involves the formation of new kamma; it is represented by designation issuing in action. Each impingent object elicits from the mind an appropriate designation, and this sparks off an action considered the fitting response. Thus the relationship between impingement and designation depicts in cognitive terms the same situation depicted in conative terms by feeling and craving: the regeneration of the round of existence through present activity building upon the kammic inheritance from the past.

The Buddha's demonstration continues by way of synthesis. Without the mental factors there could be no designation-contact, and without the material body with its sense faculties there could be no impingement-contact. Thus in the absence of both the mental body and the material body neither kind of contact could be discerned. The conclusion follows that contact is dependent on mentality-materiality, hence that mentality-materiality is the condition for contact.[14]

One puzzle posed by this passage remains. In formulating his questions, it would have been quite sufficient for the Buddha to have worded the hypothetical clause simply in terms of the absence of the intended subject, e.g. "If the mental body were absent, ..." or "If the material body were absent, ..." etc. Instead, quite uncharacteristically, he uses the more complex phrasing: "If those qualities, traits, signs, and indicators through which there is a description ... were all absent...." The question arises, then, why the Buddha resorts to this complicated mode of expression instead of using the simpler, more direct phrasing. Later developments in the sutta suggest an answer, but to discuss it we will have to wait until we come to them.

The Hidden Vortex

The next two paragraphs (§§21-22) bring the investigation of dependent arising to a climax by revealing a "hidden vortex" underlying the entire process of saṁsāric becoming.[15] This hidden vortex is the reciprocal conditionality of consciousness and mentality-materiality. The Buddha first establishes consciousness as the specific condition for mentality-materiality by demonstrating that it is indispensable to the latter at four different times: at conception, during gestation, at the time of emerging from the womb, and during the course of life (§21). Consciousness is already a condition at the moment of conception since mentality-materiality can "take shape in the womb," i.e. form into an embryo, only if consciousness has "descended into the womb." The description of consciousness as descending is metaphorical; it should not be taken literally as implying that consciousness is a self-identical entity which transmigrates from one life to another. The Buddha expressly repudiates the view that "it is this same consciousness that travels and traverses (the round of rebirths)" (M.38; i,258). Consciousness occurs by way of process. It is not an ongoing subject but a series of transitory acts of cognition arising and passing away through conditions. Each act is particular and discrete—an occasion of eye-consciousness, ear-consciousness, nose-consciousness, tongue-consciousness, body-consciousness, or mind-consciousness. Based on its sense faculty it performs its function of cognizing the object, then gives way to the next act of consciousness, which arises in immediate succession.

But though metaphorical, the phrase "descent of consciousness" makes an important point. It indicates that at conception consciousness does not arise totally anew, spontaneously, without antecedents, but occurs as a moment in a "continuum of consciousness" which has been proceeding uninterruptedly from one life to another through beginningless time. If, at the time the man and woman sexually unite, no such continuum of consciousness is available, kammically attuned to the situation, conception will not occur and there will be no formation of the embryo (M.38; i,266). In the commentaries the first occasion of consciousness in a new life is called the "rebirth-linking consciousness" (*paṭisandhiviññāṇa*). It is given this name because it "links together" the new existence with the previous one, and thereby with the entire past history of the series. Generated by a kammically formative consciousness of the previous life, it brings with it into the new life the whole stock of dispositions, character tendencies, and kamma accumulations impressed upon the continuum. At the moment the rebirth consciousness springs up in the womb, the other four aggregates comprised in mentality-materiality arise along with it. The fertilized ovum becomes the nucleus for the material body; consciousness itself directly brings along the factors of the mental body. Once locked together at conception, consciousness sustains mentality-materiality throughout the remainder of the life-span. Without it the body would collapse into a mass of lifeless matter and the mental factors would become totally defunct.

But the relationship between the two is not one-sided. To show this, the Buddha alters his regular exposition of dependent arising. Instead of taking the series back as usual to volitional formations and ignorance, he reverses his last statement and says: "With mentality-materiality as condition there is consciousness" (§22). Just as the embryo cannot form unless consciousness "descends" into the womb, so consciousness cannot initiate the new existence in the womb unless it "gains a footing" in mentality-materiality. Further, consciousness requires mentality-materiality not only at conception, but all throughout life. It depends on a vital functioning body with its brain, nervous system, and sense faculties. It also depends on the mental body, as there can be no cognition of an object without the more specialized functions performed by contact, feeling, perception, volition, attention, and the rest. Thus consciousness stands upon the whole complex of mentality-materiality, subject to the latter's fluctuations: "With the arising of mentality-materiality consciousness arises, with the ceasing of mentality-materiality consciousness ceases" (S.XXII,56; iii,61).

This disclosure of the essential interdependence of consciousness and mentality-materiality has momentous consequences for religious and philosophical thought. It provides the philosophical "middle way" between the views of eternalism and annihilationism, the two extremes which polarize man's thinking on the nature of his being. Each side of the conditioning relationship, while balancing the other, at the same time cancels out one of the two extremes by correcting its underlying error.

The declaration that consciousness depends on mentality-materiality counters the extreme of eternalism, the supposition that the person contains an indestructible, unchanging essence that can be regarded as a permanent self. Of all man's faculties, it is consciousness that most readily lends itself to the eternalist assumption, for a reason not difficult to understand. Eveything within experience is seen to change, but the knowing of change remains constant and thus (to the reflective worlding) seems to require a constant knower, one who knows but does not change. This changeless knower must be the most fundamental factor in the act of knowing, and consciousness appears to fulfil this role best. For in reflection the other faculties, bodily and mental, all point to consciousness as their mainstay and support, while consciousness does not point to anything more basic than itself. Thus consciousness is cast in the role of the changeless self-existent subject, to be seized upon by the eternalist philosopher as the transcendental ego, by the religious thinker as the immortal soul.[16] Once consciousness is so apotheosized, the other factors of the personality come to be regarded as its appendages, limiting adjuncts which obscure its intrinsic purity. From this the conclusion is drawn that if consciousness could only be separated from its appendages it would abide forever in its own eternal essence—for the monistic thinker as the universal self or the undifferentiated absolute, for the theist as the purified soul ready for union with God. To achieve this separation then becomes the goal of spiritual endeavour, approached via the religious system's specific disciplines.

The Buddha's revelation of the dependent nature of consciousness pulls the ground away from all idealistic attempts to make it an eternal self. In his own quest for enlightenment the Buddha-to-be refused to stop with consciousness as an impenetrable final term of inquiry. After he had pursued the sequence of conditions back to consciousness, he asked one further question, a question which for his time must have been incredibly bold: "What is the condition for consciousness?" And the answer came: "Then, bhikkhus, through methodical attention I comprehended with wisdom: 'When there is mentality-materiality consciousness comes to be. With mentality-materiality as condition there is consciousness.... This consciousness turns back from mentality-materiality, it does not go beyond' " (S.XII,65; ii,104).

Consciousness appears as an enduring subject due to lack of attention. When it is mindfully examined the appearance of lastingness is dissolved by the perception of its impermanence. Consciousness constantly arises and falls, and each new arising occurs through conditions: "In many ways the Exalted One has said that consciousness is dependently arisen. Apart from conditions there is no origination of consciousness" (M.38; i,258). In every phase of its being consciousness is dependent on its adjuncts, without which it could not stand: "Bhikkhus, though some recluse or brahmin might say: 'Apart from material form, apart from feeling, apart from perception, apart from mental formations, I will describe the coming and going of consciousness, its passing away and re-arising, its growth, development, and maturation'—that is impossible" (M.102; ii,230). Consciousness "turns back" from mentality-materiality and "does not go beyond" in that it does not reach back to an absolute and indestructible mode of being. Far from releasing consciousness into eternity, the removal of mentality-materiality brings only the end of consciousness itself: "With the cessation of mentality-materiality consciousness ceases." For this reason, instead of seizing upon consciousness as the inalienable core of his being, the noble disciple of the Buddha contemplates it in a different light: "Whatever there is included in consciousness, he considers it as impermanent, as suffering, as a disease, a blister or a dart, as misery, as affliction, as alien, as disintegrating, as non-self" (M.64; i,435).

Taken by itself, the statement that consciousness is dependent upon mentality-materiality (especially materiality) might be understood to suggest the nihilistic view that individual existence utterly terminates at death. For if consciousness requires the living body as support, and the body perishes with death, it would seem to follow that death brings the end of consciousness. There would then be no kammic efficacy of action, no fruition of good and evil deeds, and thus no solid basis for morality. To counter this error, the other proposition has to be taken into account: "With consciousness as condition there is mentality-materiality." Consciousness commences each existence. It is the first and primary factor which sets the new life going and without it conception could not occur at all. Consciousness is compared to the seed for the generation of new existence (A.III,76; i,223), and this comparison gives us the key for understanding its indispensable role. Just as the seed which sprouts into a young tree must come from a previous tree, so the "seed" of consciousness which starts the new life must come from consciousness in a previous life. What drives consciousness from one existence to another are the defilements of ignorance and craving; what gives it direction, determining it to particular forms of existence, are the volitions constituting kamma. These conditions brought consciousness from the past life into the present life, and as long as they remain operative they will propel it into a future life. The continuum of consciousness will again spring up established on a new physical base, and in that continuum kamma will find the field to bear its fruits. When the reciprocal conditionality of consciousness and its psychophysical adjuncts is properly understood, neither eternalism nor annihilationism can win assent.

Thus, locked in their vertical interplay, consciousness and mentality-materiality support each other, feed each other, and drive each other on, generating out of their union the whole series of dependently arisen states ending in aging and death. No matter how far back the round is traced into the past the same situation prevails: one will find only consciousness and mentality-materiality in mutual dependence, infected by ignorance and craving—never a first point when they began, never a time before which they were not. Again, no matter how far forward the round continues into the future, it will still be constituted by the same pair bound together as reciprocal conditions. The two in union are at once the ground of all existence and the "stuff" of all existence. In any attempt to explain the round they are the final terms of explanation.

This is the purport of the Buddha's words (§22): "It is to this extent that one can be born, age, and die, pass away and re-arise ... to this extent that the round turns for describing this state of being, that is, when there is mentality-materiality together with consciousness." The subcommentary succinctly conveys the sense of this statement in its gloss on the phrase "to this extent" ("by this much"): "Not through anything else besides this, through a self having the intrinsic nature of a subject or agent or through a creator God, etc." (p. 89).

The Pathway for Designation

The concluding sentence of §22 contains another statement whose implications and connection with the discourse as a whole require exploration: "(it is) to this extent that there is a pathway for designation, to this extent that there is a pathway for language, to this extent that there is a pathway for description, ... that is, when there is mentality-materiality together with consciousness." As usual, the first step in unravelling the meaning is the elucidation of terms. "Designation" (*adhivacana*), "language" (*nirutti*), and "description" (*paññatti*), according to the subcommentary, are near synonyms signifying, with minor differences of nuance, verbal statements expressive of meaning. The "pathway" (*patha*) for designation, language, and description is the domain to which they apply, their objective basis. This, the commentary says, is the same in all three cases—the five aggregates, spoken of here as "mentality-materiality together with consciousness."[17] Thus the passage can be taken to concern, in some elliptical way, the relation between concepts, language, and reality. But still the question remains as to the relevance of this to an exposition of the round.

To bring that relevance to light it is necessary to investigate briefly the nature of reference, the act which establishes connections between words and things. Designation, language, and description are the tools of reference, enabling us to interpret and evaluate our experience privately to ourselves and to communicate our thoughts to others. These tools of reference require referents. As means of designating, discussing, and describing, they necessarily point beyond themselves to a world of referents which they designate, discuss, and describe. That world is "the pathway for designation, language, and description." But reference involves more than simply the indicating of a referent. It also involves signification, the ascribing of meaning to the referent. While the referent provides the locus for meaning, the meaning itself is contributed by the mind making the reference. The section on contact should be recalled, where it was shown that designation depends upon the mental body.[18] It is in the mental body that designations, linguistic expressions, and descriptions take shape, and from there that they are ascribed, end-products of a complex process drawing upon the contributions of many individual mental factors.

Like photographs turned out by a camera, the conceptual and verbal symbols that issue from the mental body can be no more accurate in representing actuality than the instrument which creates them is accurate in recording actuality. Distortion occurring in the process of cognition is bound to infiltrate the act of reference and leave its mark upon the conceptual scheme through which experience is interpreted. When feeling is seized upon as food for desire, when perception becomes a scanning device for finding pleasure and avoiding threats to the ego, when volition is driven by greed and hate and attention flits about unsteadily, one can hardly expect the mental body to mirror the world "as it really is" in flawlessly precise concepts and expressions. To the contrary, the system of references that results will be a muddled one, reflecting the individual's biases, presuppositions, and wayward emotions as much as the things they refer to. Even when the assignment of meanings to terms conforms to the conventions governing their use, that is no guarantee against aberrant references; for often these conventions stem from and reinforce unrecognized common error, the "collective hallucinations" of the world.

Of all the tools of reference a person may use, those of greatest importance to himself are the ones that enable him to establish and confirm his sense of his own identity. These are the designations "mine," "I am," and "my self." In the Buddha's teaching such ideas and all related notions, in the way they are ordinarily entertained, are regarded as conceptual expressions of the ego-consciousness. They are fabrications of the mind (*mathita*), subjective conceivings (*maññita*), conceptual proliferations (*papañcita*) grounded in ignorance, craving, and clinging. But the "uninstructed worldling" (*assutavā puthujjana*), the individual unlearned and untrained in the Buddha's teaching, does not even suspect their falsity. Not knowing that their real origins are purely internal, he assumes they simply duplicate in thought what exists as concrete fact. Thus he takes them to possess objectively the meaning he ascribes to them, as standing for a self and its belongings. Caught up in his own deception, he then makes use of these notions as instruments of appropriation and identification. Through the designation "mine" he establishes a territory over which he claims control, through the designations "I am" and "my self" he establishes an identity upon which he builds his conceits and views.

The objects of these conceptual and verbal manipulations are the five aggregates. These are the referents, the "pathway for designation," to which the worldling's references necessarily refer: "There being material form, feeling, perception, mental formations, and consciousness, bhikkhus, it is referring to them, adhering to them (*upādāya abhinivissa*), that one considers 'This is mine, this I am, this is my self'" (S.XXII,150; iii,181-83). Correct designation requires that the referent be designated without overshooting its real nature by attributing to it some significance it does not have. But the worldling's cognitive processes, being under the dominion of ignorance, do not present things as they are in themselves. They present them in distorted forms fashioned by the defilements at work behind his cognition. Therefore, when he refers to the referents in thought and speech, his references are loaded with a charge of meaning deriving from their subjective roots. In his reflection upon his immediate experience he does not see simply material form, feeling, perception, mental formations, and consciousness. He reads his designations into the referents and comes up with: "Material form which is mine, which I am. Feeling ... perception ... mental formations ... consciousness which is mine, which I am" (see S.XXII,1; iii,3-4).

Since the worldling already sees a self when he considers his experience analytically, when he encounters dependent arising—which describes experience dynamically—he inevitably views it through the same distorting lens:

> (The Exalted One said:) "With the six sense bases as condition contact comes to be."—"Venerable sir, who makes contact?"—"Not a proper question. I do not say 'One makes contact.' If I

> should say 'One makes contact,' it would be proper to ask: 'Who makes contact?' But I do not say this. Since I do not say this the proper question to ask me is: 'Through what condition does contact come to be?' To this the proper answer is: 'With the six sense bases as condition contact comes to be. With contact as condition feeling comes to be.'"—"Venerable sir, who feels?" (S.XII.12; ii,13)

So it goes on, all the way down the line. He sees *someone* who craves, who clings, who exists, who is born, who ages, who dies. He holds: "Aging and death are one thing, the one to whom they occur is another. Birth is one thing, the one to whom it occurs is another" (S.XII,35; ii,61). For him the whole vortical interplay of consciousness and mentality-materiality seems to revolve around a stable centre, the "who" to whom it is happening. What he does not see and cannot see, as long as he remains immersed in his assumptions, is: "to this extent the round turns for describing this state of being, that is, when there is mentality-materiality together with consciousness."

With this we come upon the reason why the Buddha declares dependent arising to be so deep and difficult to understand. It is deep and difficult not simply because it describes the causal pattern governing the round, but because it describes that pattern in terms of bare conditions and conditioned phenomena without reference to a self. The challenge is to see that whatever happens in the course of existence is merely a conditioned event happening through conditions in a continuum of dependently arisen phenomena. It is not happening *to* anyone. There is no agent behind the actions, no knower behind the knowing, no transmigrating self passing through the round. What binds the factors of experience together, at any given moment and from moment to moment, is the principle of dependent arising itself: "When there is this, that comes to be; with the arising of this, that arises." This itself is sufficient because this by itself is adequate and complete.

By pointing to the juncture of consciousness and mentality-materiality as the pathway for designation, language, and description, the Buddha delimits the final domain of reference as the phenomena comprised in dependent arising. All concepts, words, and linguistic expressions emerge from these and all ultimately refer back to them. This includes such designations as "mine," "I," and "self," as well as the more elaborate verbal formulations employing them. Though such terms seem to imply a self as their referent, if that self is sought for it cannot be found. All that is found as the final referents are the five aggregates, and when these are methodically examined they fail to exhibit the qualities that would qualify them as self. Selfhood implies permanence, autonomy, and mastery over things; the five aggregates all turn out to be impermanent, conditioned, and unmasterable.

However, though a self and its belongings cannot be discovered, the conclusion does not follow that such words as "mine," "I," and "self" are to be proscribed. These words and their derivatives have a perfectly legitimate, even necessary, use as tools of communication. They are index terms for referring to situations too complex for full descriptions phrased exclusively in terms of "bare phenomena." The Buddha and his disciples use them in their speech as freely as anyone else; but when used by them these terms do not betray underlying attitudes of craving, conceit, and wrong views, as is generally the case with their employment by others. For them the terms are entirely divested of their subjective overtones, used with a recognition of their purely referential function: "These, Citta, are merely names, expressions, turns of speech, designations in common use in the world. And of these a Tathāgata makes use, indeed, but he does not misapprehend them" (D.9; i,201-2).

The foregoing discussion suggests an answer to a puzzle mentioned earlier but left unresolved—that concerning the Buddha's manner of formulating his questions about the conditions for contact (see above, p. 17). The complex phrasing may be taken to imply a distinction between two kinds of entities: the fully actual phenomena pertaining to the "pathways for designation, language, and description" and the mental constructs derivative upon them.[19] The fully actual phenomena are things endowed with their own intrinsic natures (*sabhāva*); that is, the five aggregates. These things exist quite independently of conceptualization. They might be apprehended in thought and designated and described by words, but they do not depend upon thought and verbal expression for their being. They acquire being through their own conditions, which are other fully actual phenomena. Mental constructs, in contrast, have no being apart from conceptual formulation. They do not possess intrinsic natures but exist solely in the realm of thought and ideation. They refer to actual phenomena and their components invariably derive from them, since the fully actual phenomena are the foundation and building blocks for all mental construction. But to form the construct, the given data have been pressed through various conceptual operations such as abstraction, synthesis, and imaginative embellishment. Consequently, the finished product is often difficult to trace back to its experiential originals.

The criterion for distinguishing the two is implied by the sutta's phrase "those qualities, traits, signs, and indicators through which there is a description of the mental (material) body." As things endowed with intrinsic natures, fully actual phenomena reveal their natures through certain characteristics, which are discovered as objective features of the world. By way of these characteristics—"those qualities," etc.—the phenomena are experienced immediately as objects of direct cognition, and this cognition validates their reality as things existing independently of conceptualization. The mental constructs, on the other hand, do not reveal their own distinctive "qualities, traits, signs, and indicators." Though they may be ascribed to the world as if they were fully actual, all attempts to locate them within the world through directly cognizable characteristics eventually turn out to be futile. Investigation always leads, on one side, to the mental processes responsible for the construction; on the other, to the "pathways" which provide the raw materials and the objective basis to which the completed constructs are ascribed.

The same passage also suggests certain principles regarding description. It implies that "veridical description," i.e. description true from the special standpoint of insight-contemplation, not only represents actuality correctly, but represents it solely in terms of what is discovered in contemplation—its constituent phenomena, their qualities, and their relations. Examples would be such statements as: "The earth element has the characteristic of hardness, consciousness that of cognizing an object," etc.; or "All material form is impermanent," etc.; or "Craving arises with feeling as condition," etc. Such description may be distinguished from "deviant description," which either posits mental constructs as actual existents (a Creator God, the world spirit, the personal soul, the absolute, etc.), or else ascribes to the actual phenomena attributes they only appear to possess due to cognitive distortion. The most important of these, from the standpoint of the Dhamma, are the appearances of beauty, pleasure, permanence, and self (*subha, sukha, nicca, attā*). The relevance of this distinction to the sutta will become clear later, when we come to the section on descriptions of self.

The pathways for designation, language, and description are not all that the vortical interplay of consciousness and mentality-materiality makes possible. The Buddha says that it also makes possible a sphere for wisdom (*paññāvacara*). The sphere for wisdom is the pathways themselves: the five aggregates in process of dependent arising. As long as the aggregates are enveloped by ignorance, they become the basis for conceiving the deluded notions "mine," "I am," and "my self." But when they are examined with mindfulness and clear comprehension, they become transformed into the soil for the growth of wisdom. Wisdom works with the same set of referents as deluded conceptualization—the five aggregates, etc.—but exhibits them from a new point of view, one which leads to the abolition of all conceivings: "Whatever material form there is, whatever feeling, perception, mental formations, and consciousness—past, future, or present, internal or external, gross or subtle, inferior or superior, far or near—all that one sees with perfect wisdom as it really is: 'This is not mine, this I am not, this is not my self.' For one knowing and seeing thus, there are no more ego-conceptions, conceptions of 'mine,' and underlying tendencies to conceit in regard to this conscious body and all external signs'" (S.XII,91; iii,136).

Descriptions of Self

In the next section of the sutta (§23) the Buddha seems to divert the discussion to a new topic apparently unrelated to the foregoing exposition. The commentary clarifies the movement of the discourse by pointing out that this new section refers back to the Buddha's original statement that "this generation has become like a tangled skein." The purpose is to elucidate this statement by identifying the tangles and showing how the process of entanglement has taken place. Thus the discussion is still concerned with the causal structure of the round, only now it approaches that structure from a different angle.

The reason "this generation has become like a tangled skein" is its failure to understand and penetrate dependent arising. The non-penetration of dependent arising is an aspect of ignorance, and ignorance (as the usual twelvefold formula shows) is the most fundamental condition for the round of becoming. Thus the basic factor responsible for the continued movement of dependent arising is the non-penetration of dependent arising itself. Or, to state the matter in different words, what keeps beings in bondage to the round is their own lack of insight into the conditioning process that keeps them bound.

Ignorance is a state of privation, an absence of true knowledge: knowledge of the Four Noble Truths, of dependent arising, of the three characteristics of phenomena. But the mind, like nature, cannot tolerate a vacuum. So when true knowledge is lacking, something else in the guise of knowledge moves in to take its place. What moves in are views (*diṭṭhi*). Views are erroneous opinions about the nature of the world, personal existence, and the way to deliverance. They range from simple unexamined assumptions to formulated doctrines, to theories and speculations, to elaborate systems of belief. Views generally pose as detached, sober, rational attempts at understanding ultimate issues.

Behind views of self - an enormously powerful investment of emotion the emotion comes from craving.

But beneath this pose they create a tremendous amount of trouble—confusion within and conflicts without. In their vast diversity, their lack of sound foundations, their internal contradictions and mutual incompatibility, views give little ground for confidence. That is why, in adhering to them, "this generation has become like a tangled skein." Views are the tangles, knots, and matting in the works that prevent living beings from passing beyond saṁsāra.

Earlier it was said that of all the designations a person uses, those most important to himself are the ones that confirm his sense of his own identity. By the same token, of the numerous views a person may hold, those held to with the greatest tenacity are his views of self, which define for him that identity. The Buddha has shown that behind these views of self lies an enormously powerful investment of emotion. The emotion comes from craving, and when it is invested in a particular view it turns that view into an instrument of clinging. Thus an examination of views of self, far from diverting the discussion from dependent arising, actually focuses it in more closely upon a specific factor in the sequence of conditions—namely, upon clinging in its mode of "clinging to a doctrine of self" (*attavād'upādāna*). In this mode clinging takes on a role of critical importance, for it represents that point in the unfolding of the conditions where ignorance and craving—in themselves blind forces—acquire an intellectual justification. They join up with the intellect to create for themselves a conceptualized view of self, which protects them with a semblance of rationality. Therefore, in order to dislodge ignorance and craving, a preliminary step often becomes necessary: to take away their protective shield of views.

The Buddha begins his examination of views of self by laying out the different descriptions of self (*attapaññatti*) proposed by speculative thinkers. The title of the section and the frequent use of the word "describes" (*paññāpeti*) connect this discussion with earlier ones on description. In the closing statement of §22 the Buddha drew the boundaries to the domain of description as the five aggregates, implying that it is in terms of these factors that all legitimate description is formulated. The passage on contact (§20) suggested that veridical description, valid from the viewpoint of insight-contemplation, describes the world strictly in terms of its fully actual phenomena, their qualities, and their relations. Now, in this section on descriptions of self, the Buddha will show what happens when these stipulations are neglected, when thought oversteps its bounds and runs wild in the wilderness of its own conceivings.

Descriptions of self are the outcome of the worldling's attempt to

+ when it is invested in a particular view + turns that view into an instrument of clinging

work out a reflective interpretation of his existence. This task he invariably approaches by speculating about his self. Depending on his personal predilections, reasoning, and experience, he formulates (or adopts) a particular conception of self, then blows this up into a full-fledged theory accounting for its origins, destiny, and relations to the world. Not content simply to define his views to himself, he seeks to gain acceptance of them from others. Thus, to win adherents, he devises detailed descriptions of the self, offers arguments in favour of his doctrine, and tries to discredit the doctrines of his rivals.

In various suttas the Buddha has surveyed the results of speculative thought, the fullest treatment being the Brahmajāla Sutta with its sixty-two views on the self and the world. In the present sutta he reduces this diversity to twelve views consisting of four primary positions each capable of appearing in three different modes. After explaining all the views the Buddha does not attempt to dispose of them with individual refutations. Such an approach does not generate genuine understanding; moreover, it would involve him in the same "scuffling of views," the doctrinal quarrels and contentions, he exhorts his own disciples to avoid. Instead of grappling with theoretical formulations, he pursues the adherence to views of self down to a more fundamental level where the speculative enterprise originates.

The worldling's endeavour to understand his existence always turns into speculations on self because he carries into his systematic thinking the everyday presupposition that self is the basic truth of his existence. This presupposition he accepts prior to and quite apart from all serious reflection; indeed he does not even recognize it as a presupposition, for the reason that he perceives a self as inherent in his experience. Conceptually he tries to pinpoint this self in relation to the experiential situation, and this results in "considerations of self," which become the pre-speculative basis for his more systematic "descriptions of self." The Buddha's method of dealing with views in this sutta is to pass directly from the descriptions of self to the underlying considerations. He sets forth the alternative ways of considering self, examines them, and shows that none can stand up under scrutiny. When all possible ways of considering self are seen to be defective, logic leads back to the conclusion (not explicitly drawn in the sutta) that none of the descriptions of self is tenable.

The section on descriptions of self prepares the way for the Buddha's critique by exhibiting the speculative views of self in their mutual opposition (§23). The commentary explains that these views can arise either from meditative experience or from bare reasoning. In the case where they arise from meditative experience, the commentary treats them (perhaps too narrowly) as originating from misinterpretations of the "kasiṇa sign," the inwardly visualized image of the meditation object. If the sign itself is apprehended as self, self will be conceived as material; if the area covered by the sign, or the mental factors contemplating it, is apprehended, self will be conceived as immaterial. If the sign is unextended, i.e. confined to a small area, self will be conceived as limited; if the sign is extended as far as visualization will allow, self will be conceived as infinite. Permutation of these paired alternatives yields four primary ways of describing self.

Having determined the nature of self, the theorist next considers its future destiny (§24), an issue of vital importance to himself as it concerns the fate of his cherished identity. Temporal speculations admit of three possibilities, which in principle can be combined with any of the four basic views.[20] The first two are clear: the annihilationist view (*ucchedavāda*) that the self exists only in the present life and utterly perishes at death, and the eternalist view (*sassatavāda*) that the self continues permanently into the future. The third proposition is perplexing even in the Pali; the translation given in the text below renders it as literally as possible. The commentary interprets the statement as indicating the dispute between the annihilationist and the eternalist: each declares his intention to convert his opponent to his own viewpoint. But as the context requires a third view of the future of the self, an alternative interpretation might be suggested. Perhaps the passage can be taken to express the view that eternal existence is something the self must acquire. On this view the self is not everlasting by nature, but by making the appropriate effort it can be raised from transience to eternity. However, in the absence of corroboration from other sources, this interpretation must remain hypothetical.

In the sutta the Buddha does not explicitly criticize these speculations, but his statement about the pathway for description is enough to indicate where the theorists have gone astray. The descriptive content of their assertions is perfectly legitimate, as it draws entirely on what is given within experience: material and immaterial phenomena, limited and extended kasiṇa signs, present existence and future existence. The error lies in the ascription of this content to a self and in the consequent postulation of self's eternal existence or annihilation. With that step description has deviated from its proper pathway, for what is discovered within experience has been used to describe what can never be discovered but only presupposed—an unjustifiable move. The theorist, however, does not recognize his mistake. Because he starts with a "settled view of self," whatever he encounters, whether in his reasonings or his meditative attainments, will only go to confirm his preconception. In this way an unexamined assumption at an earlier stage becomes the basis for a firmly grasped error at a later stage.

A short section on "non-descriptions of self" (§25-26) is included to contrast the speculative theorists with the followers of the Buddha's teaching, who on the basis of their own attainments, learning, or practice refrain from proposing descriptions of self. The key to this section is a sentence from the commentary: "They know that the counterpart sign of the kasiṇa is only a counterpart sign and that the immaterial aggregates are only immaterial aggregates." That is, they keep their descriptions well within the range of the describable. They do not overstep the limits by ascribing to real things an unreal significance, such as selfhood, eternal existence, or annihilation. If they describe their attainments in meditation, they describe them in terms of what is found by direct cognition: a constellation of dependently arisen phenomena all impermanent, suffering, and not-self.

Considerations of Self

Descriptions of self arise because, in his non-theoretical moments, the theorist engages in considerations of self (*attasamanupassanā*). Both the descriptions and considerations are views, but the considerations occupy a more rudimentary stage on the scale of subjectivity. Descriptions of self involve a high degree of reflection: they theorize about a self, speculate over its destiny, advance reasoned arguments and proofs. Considerations of self are not entirely unreflective, but the reflection that enters into them lacks the elaborateness and refinement of the descriptions. Their basic function is to substantiate the idea of self by relating it to the given content of experience. For this reason the considerations of self are far more widespread than the descriptions. Few try to work out systematic views about the self, but almost everyone—whether commoner or philosopher—cherishes some notion about what he is beneath his names and forms. That notion is his consideration of self.

The problem of finding some identity for the self arises because the worldling continually conceives his experience through the filter of the notion "I am." This notion—called a conceit (*māna*), a desire (*chanda*), and an underlying tendency (*anusaya*), but not a view (see S.XXII,89; iii,130)—arises spontaneously in his mind due to the basic ignorance. The worldling accepts the idea "I am" as indicating what it seems to indicate, a self. "Self" is the notion of a truly existent "I," an "I" which is not a mere referential designation but an enduring centre of personal identity. The worldling embraces this idea of self as an overwhelming certainty; at the same time, however, it remains for him an enigma. Self is his identity, what he really is at the core of his being, yet it never reveals *its own* identity, freely and openly, to direct cognition. Its identity is always something that has to be figured out, "squeezed" out of the data by deduction and inference, not something clearly self-manifesting. However, since the worldling finds the idea of self unimpeachable, he feels it must have some identity, and thus (without quite being aware that he is doing so) he proceeds to give it one.

To provide the self with an identity he must make use of the material available to him for consideration, and that is the five aggregates. Thus all considerations of self are formulated with reference to the aggregates: "Those recluses and brahmins, bhikkhus, who considering self consider it in various ways, all consider the five aggregates or a certain one of them" (S.XXII,47; iii,46). Since the five aggregates constitute the person (*sakkāya*), the view of a self existing in relation to the aggregates is called "personality view" (*sakkāyadiṭṭhi*). Personality view can assume twenty forms, arrived at by conceiving self in four ways relative to each aggregate: "Herein, bhikkhu, an uninstructed worldling, who is without regard for the noble ones … considers material form as self, or self as possessing material form, or material form as in self, or self as in material form. He considers feeling … perception … mental formations … consciousness as self, or self as possessing consciousness, or consciousness as in self, or self as in consciousness. Thus, bhikkhu, there is personality view" (S.XXII,82; iii,102).

With personality view the indeterminate "I am" receives a determinate identity. It is transformed into the designation "this I am," where the "this" represents the content the aggregates provide for identifying the conceptually vacuous "I."[21] Once the "I" is defined in thought, speculation takes over to elaborate more specific views about its past and future and other matters of vital concern. Thus all speculative flights on the self's nature and destiny begin with the inherent tendency to conceive the person as self. If speculative views be regarded as the knots that bind the worldling to the round, personality view can be considered the rope:

> Bhikkhus, this saṁsāra is without conceivable beginning. No first point is discerned of beings roaming and wandering (in saṁsāra), hindered by ignorance and fettered by craving. Just as a dog, teth-

> ered by a leash and tied to a stout pole or post, keeps running and circling around that same pole or post, in the same way, bhikkhus, the uninstructed worldling, who is without regard for the noble ones ... considers material form as self ... or self as in consciousness. He keeps running and circling around that same material form, that same feeling, that same perception, those same mental formations, that same consciousness. Running and circling thus, he is not released from material form, feeling, perception, mental formations, and consciousness; he is not released from birth, aging and death, from sorrow, lamentation, pain, grief, and despair, he is not released from suffering, I declare. (S.XXII,99; iii,150)

In the Mahānidāna Sutta the Buddha does not investigate the whole gamut of personality view in all its twenty forms. Instead he selects one aggregate, the aggregate of feeling, as representative of the lot and then examines three alternative ways in which it can be made a basis for conceiving self. One who recognizes a self either considers feeling as self, or considers self as altogether without feeling, or considers self as distinct from but subject to feeling (§27). According to the commentary, the second is the view that self is matter, the third the view that self is a combination of the other three mental aggregates.[22] This stipulation suggests certain connections with the developed descriptions of self: the first and third considerations lead to the description of self as immaterial, the second to the description of self as "having material form."

As these three formulations are exhaustive, when the Buddha shows them all to be unacceptable the view of self is left without a foothold. It should be pointed out, however, that the Buddha does not refute the three views with independent lines of argument. He employs the method of *reductio ad absurdum.* Starting with the theorist's own premises, he shows that if the implications of his position are clearly spelled out, it leads to consequences he himself would not be willing to accept. Thus the Buddha's demonstration undermines each view from within itself; or rather, it shows that each view is already undermined from within itself by its own implicit internal contradictions.

The Buddha examines first the view that feeling is self (§§28-29). The theorist who asserts this view is asked to state *which* kind of feeling he considers as self: pleasant feeling, painful feeling, or neither-pleasant-nor-painful feeling.[23] These three kinds of feeling are distinct and mutually exclusive. Only one can be experienced at a time. Thus when one kind of feeling has arisen, the other two are necessarily absent. Calling attention to this diversity in feeling already deals a blow to the notion of self. It exposes feeling as a succession of distinct states lacking the enduring identity essential to selfhood.

If feeling is self, whatever attributes belong to feeling also belong to self and whatever happens to feeling also happens to self. Since feeling is impermanent, conditioned, dependently arisen, and subject to destruction, it would follow that the same pertains to self. This is a conclusion the theorist could not accept, as it contradicts his conception of self as permanent, unconditioned, independent, and indestructible; yet his initial thesis forces it upon him. Further, all feeling ceases and disappears, so if one identifies a particular feeling as self, with the ceasing of that feeling one would have to assert that self has disappeared—for the theorist an unthinkable situation, as it would leave him without the self he is seeking to establish.

The theorist might try to salvage his position by refusing to tie self down to particular feelings. Instead he regards feeling in general as self. But this position leads to snags of its own. Self would still be impermanent, as with the breakup of each feeling self would undergo dissolution. As the qualities of selfhood must attach to all feelings, the three mutually exclusive feelings would have to share the permanence attributed to self. Thus all feelings would somehow exist at all times and self would be a compound of different feelings, an impossible conclusion. Moreover, as feeling is observed to constantly arise and pass away, self would do so likewise, in direct contradiction to the unstated premise that selfhood necessarily excludes arising and passing away.[24] Therefore, as self would turn out to be "impermanent, a mixture of pleasure and pain, and subject to arising and falling away," the view that feeling is self is unacceptable.

The second view, which asserts self to be altogether without experience of feeling, the commentary identifies as the view that self is bare material form. The Buddha rejects the view of a completely insentient self on the ground that such a self could not even conceive the idea "I am" (§30). The argument is based on the theorist's presupposition (again unstated) that selfhood requires some degree of self-consciousness. Ascribing selfhood to something which cannot affirm its own existence as a self defeats the very purpose of claiming selfhood. The dependency of the idea "I am" on feeling implicitly refers back to the section on contact (§20). Feeling is part of the mental body, and without the factors of the mental body designation-contact (in this case, the designation "I am") cannot occur in the material body. A material body without feeling does not affirm self and thus cannot be self; it remains only a mass of matter.

The third view attempts to avoid the faults of the first two positions by making self the subject of feeling (§31). As on this view self remains distinct from feeling, the impermanence of feeling need not undermine the permanency of self. As self undergoes feelings, the absurdity of a totally insentient self is sidestepped. This position in effect establishes a dualism of self and the psychophysical faculties as its adjuncts. The self cannot be reduced to the adjuncts and thus does not share their vicissitudes; but it enters into union with them and through them experiences the world. Perhaps the closest historical parallel to this view is the Sāṅkhya philosophy with its dualism of *puruṣa*, the self as the changeless witness of nature, and *prakṛti*, nature itself, the ever-changing psychophysical field.

Though more promising at first than the other two positions, this position too turns out to be flawed. Fundamental to the notion of selfhood is an inherent capacity for self-affirmation; as the autonomous subject of experience, self should be able to affirm its own being and identity to itself without need for external referents. Yet, the theorist is forced to admit that, with the cessation of feeling, in the complete absence of feeling, the idea "I am this" could not be conceived. The assumed self can only identify itself as "this," e.g. "I am the experiencer of feeling," by reference to its psychophysical adjuncts. If these are removed, all points of reference for self to conceive its identity are removed and it then becomes a conceptual cipher. Again, the earlier statement should be recalled: without mentality-materiality together with consciousness there is no pathway for designation. When the referents are withdrawn, the designation "I am this" vanishes.

It is no use trying to dismiss the Buddha's rhetorical question as irrelevant on the ground that the clause about feeling ceasing "absolutely and utterly" is purely hypothetical and feeling can continue forever. For whether or not feeling does in fact ever cease absolutely is immaterial. The question clinches the point that the supposed self, being incapable of identifying itself without reference to its adjuncts, becomes totally dependent upon them for its identity—a strange predicament for an autonomous self to get into. Moreover, as the adjuncts it depends on for its identity are impermanent and conditioned, it becomes impossible to maintain the permanency and unconditionedness of self. But an impermanent and conditioned self is not a self at all, but a contradiction in terms. Thus once again, beginning with the theorist's own unstated premises, the assertion of self turns out to be inadmissible. Since all three positions are internally contradictory yet exhaustive of all possible views on self, the only escape route from the impasse is to reject the notion of selfhood altogether. Far from being a gesture of despair at the end of a blind alley, this relinquishing of all conceptions of self turns out to be a step through the door to liberation.

Thus the Buddha passes from exposing the flaws in considerations of self to demonstrating how a bhikkhu who abandons all these considerations attains arahatship (§32). The commentary says that the bhikkhu is one who practises meditation on the foundations of mindfulness (*satipaṭṭhāna*). Since feeling was used to expound the views sustaining the round, we may presume that the bhikkhu strives to develop insight by practising the contemplation of feeling (*vedanānupassanā*). He discerns the rise and fall of feeling, sees all feelings as stamped with the three characteristics of impermanence, suffering, and non-self, and so refrains from conceiving self in relation to feeling. Passing on to the contemplation of phenomena (*dhammānupassanā*), he extends his insight into the three characteristics from feeling to all the five aggregates. Whatever he contemplates from among the aggregates, he considers: "This is not mine, this I am not, this is not my self." When his insight comes to maturity he cuts off clinging and attains nibbāna here and now.

Such a bhikkhu, established in arahatship, does not affirm any of the four standard views on the status of a Tathāgata after death. A Tathāgata here is a perfected individual, one who has reached the final goal. In the philosophical circles of the Buddha's time, all thinkers of standing were expected to define the condition of the Perfect One after death, and these pronouncements had to fit into the tetralemma. But the Buddha refused to endorse any of the four positions. The reason is not merely that he regarded them as idle speculations not conducive to spiritual edification. This is part of the reason, the best known part, but it is not the whole story. In rejecting the four views the Buddha says, in regard to each, that "it does not apply," and this statement implies that there is a philosophical consideration behind his silence, not merely a practical one. The most fundamental reason for which the Buddha rejects the entire tetralemma is that all four positions share a common error: the assumption that a Tathāgata exists as a self. Thus their formulations veer towards the speculative extremes. The view that a Tathāgata exists after death is eternalism; the view that he does not exist after death is annihilationism; the third and fourth positions are, respectively, a syncretism and agnosticism grounded upon the same assumption. For the Enlightened One, who has seen the arising and passing away of the five aggregates, all ego-conceptions, conceptions of "mine," and underlying tendencies to conceit have been abandoned.

Thus, with the uprooting of all conceivings, he does not even see a self-existent Tathāgata to die, let alone to be eternalized or annihilated after death.[25]

The same reason for maintaining a "noble silence" applies to the arahat bhikkhu described in the sutta. But here the reason is stated more obliquely: that he has directly known "the extent of designation and the extent of the pathway for designation," etc. In the light of the earlier discussion, the meaning of this passage should be clear. The liberated bhikkhu understands the distinction between the terms of reference—designations, language, and descriptions—and the "pathways" of reference, the referents comprised in the five aggregates. Understanding this distinction he cannot be led astray by such terms as "I," "mine," "self," "person," and "being." He no longer takes them as simple indicators of reality or ascribes to them a significance born from deluded cognition. He knows their proper range of application and can use them freely when needed without being trapped by them. So too with the designation "Tathāgata." The bhikkhu knows that "Tathāgata" is just a convenient term for referring to a conglomerate process of impermanent, empty phenomena which are suffering in the deepest sense. He understands that this process has arisen dependent upon conditions, that the conditions which brought it into being have been eradicated, and that with the breakup of the body the process will come to an end:

> "Friend Yamaka, if they were to question you thus: 'Friend Yamaka, with the breakup of the body, after death, what happens to the bhikkhu who is an arahat, a destroyer of the cankers?'—being thus questioned, what would you answer?"
>
> "If, friend, they were to question me thus, I would answer: 'Friends, material form is impermanent. What is impermanent is suffering. It is suffering that has ceased and passed away. Feeling ... perception ... mental formations ... consciousness is impermanent. What is impermanent is suffering. It is suffering that has ceased and passed away.'" (S.XXII,85; iii,112)

The Liberated One

Having shown the arahat in a general way, without distinctions, in the final sections of the sutta (§§33-36) the Buddha introduces a division of the liberated one into two types: the *paññāvimutta* arahat, "the one liberated by wisdom," and the *ubhatobhāgavimutta* arahat, "the one liberated in both ways." Both types achieve arahatship through wisdom, always the direct instrument for cutting off the ignorance that holds the defilements in place. For both the content of that wisdom is the same, the understanding of the Four Noble Truths. For both the eradication of defilements is equally complete and final. What distinguishes them is their facility in serenity (*samatha*): the extent to which they have gained mastery over the meditative attainments on the side of concentration (*samādhi*).

A clear sutta statement of the difference between the two types is found in the Kīṭāgiri Sutta (M.70; i,477-78). There the *ubhatobhāgavimutta* is described as a person who dwells "having suffused with the body" (*kāyena phusitvā*) the immaterial emancipations which are peaceful and transcend material form; and having seen with wisdom, his cankers are destroyed. The *paññāvimutta* does not dwell "having suffused with the body" the immaterial emancipations; but having seen with wisdom, for him too the cankers are destroyed. The distinguishing mark between them, then, is the "bodily suffusion" of the immaterial emancipations—the four immaterial attainments and the cessation of perception and feeling. The *ubhatobhāgavimutta* arahat has this experience, the *paññāvimutta* lacks it.[26] The commentary regards *ubhatobhāgavimutta* arahatship as the consummation for the person originally spoken of as "not describing self," *paññāvimutta* arahatship as the consummation for the bhikkhu who does not consider self. The reason for this connection, presumably, is that the former passage may be read as alluding to the immaterial attainments, while the latter contains no indications of any attainments in serenity.

In the sutta itself the *paññāvimutta* arahat is described in terms of his understanding of the different realms of existence. This indirect presentation gives the Buddha the opportunity to sketch the topography of saṁsāra. Already, by explaining the conditions responsible for rebirth, he has depicted the generative structure of the round. Now, by showing the planes where rebirth can take place, he draws a picture of its cosmological terrain. The planes are divided into the seven stations for consciousness and the two bases; elsewhere these are collectively called the nine abodes of beings.[27] The round, the Buddha said earlier, turns only so long as consciousness "gains a footing" in mentality-materiality. The seven stations for consciousness provide the cosmic expanse of mentality-materiality where consciousness gains that footing, establishes itself, and comes to growth.[28]

The *paññāvimutta* arahat attains liberation by understanding each of the nine planes of existence from five angles: by way of its origin, passing away, satisfaction, unsatisfactoriness, and the escape from it.[29]

The origin and passing away of the planes can be interpreted both as the conditioned origination and cessation of existence in those realms and the momentary production and dissolution of their constituent phenomena. The former interpretation, taken as a basis for contemplation, leads to the comprehension of dependent arising, the latter to insight first into impermanence and then into the other two characteristics, suffering and non-self. Contemplation of the remaining three aspects brings understanding of the Four Noble Truths: "satisfaction" implies craving, the truth of the origin of suffering, "unsatisfactoriness" the truth of suffering, "escape" the truth of cessation together with the path. When a bhikkhu understands the nine planes from these five angles, he abandons clinging and attains arahatship as one liberated by wisdom. Since he has not gained mastery over the meditative attainments (at least not the immaterial ones), it is clear he does not arrive at insight by contemplating these planes clairvoyantly. His knowledge is inductive rather than direct. By direct insight he can see that the phenomena included in his own experience have an origin and a passing away, that they yield satisfaction, are fraught with danger and misery, and that an escape from them exists. By induction he understands that these five aspects extend to all phenomena throughout all planes.

Nothing is said in the sutta itself about the *paññāvimutta* arahat's abilities on the side of serenity. The commentary, filling in, explains that this type is fivefold: the "dry-insight meditator" (*sukkhavipassaka*) who attains arahatship by the power of insight alone without the support of a fine-material-sphere jhāna, and those who reach arahatship after basing themselves on one or another of the four fine-material-sphere jhānas. The *paññāvimutta* arahat is thus certainly not bereft of achievement in serenity; to the contrary, he can carry serenity quite far. However, not being an obtainer of the eight emancipations, unable to dwell "having suffused these with the body," he lacks the power of eminent concentration.

The *ubhatobhāgavimutta* arahat, in contrast, is expressly described by way of his mastery over the eight emancipations. The emancipations (§35) include the nine successive attainments reached by the power of concentration: the four jhānas, the four immaterial attainments, and the cessation of perception and feeling. The four jhānas are not mentioned among the emancipations under their own name, but are included by the first three items in the set. These first three emancipations, besides being each inclusive of the four jhānas, as a set seem to be an abridgement of the eight "positions of mastery" (*abhibhāyatana*; see D.16; ii,110-11) The cessation of perception and feeling requires not only concentration but also insight; it can be attained only by non-returners and arahats who have already mastered the immaterial attainments. On the basis of the commentarial discussion, it seems that for a meditative attainment to qualify as an emancipation it is not enough merely that it be entered and dwelt in; rather, after being attained, it has to be developed to such a degree of eminence that it "thoroughly releases" the mind from the states opposed to it.

The commentaries explain the word *ubhatobhāgavimutta* as meaning both liberated *through* two portions and liberated *from* two portions. Through his mastery over the immaterial attainments this type of arahat is liberated from the material body, through his attainment of the path of arahatship he is liberated from the mental body. This twofold liberation of the *ubhatobhāgavimutta* arahat should not be confused (as it sometimes is) with the two liberations—"liberation of mind" (*cetovimutti*) and "liberation by wisdom" (*paññāvimutti*)—mentioned in §36. These two kinds of liberation are used to describe arahatship in general and pertain to all arahats (see M.i,35-36); they even appear in a passage describing a type of arahat expressly defined as one who does not obtain the eight emancipations (A.IV,87; ii,87). "Liberation of mind" here signifies the release of the mind from lust that takes place through the arahat's prior development of concentration, "liberation by wisdom" the release from ignorance that takes place through his development of wisdom (A.II.iii,10; i,61). In the commentaries the former is taken to denote the concentration faculty in the arahat's fruition attainment, the latter to denote the wisdom faculty.

As the *ubhatobhāgavimutta* arahat is described as one who obtains the eight emancipations, the question may be raised how far his accomplishment in this area must go to merit the title "liberated in both ways." The Kīṭāgiri Sutta cited above makes it plain that the immaterial emancipations are necessary. But need he obtain all these without omission? The exegetical texts answer in the negative. The commentary says that the "one liberated in both ways" is fivefold by way of those who attain arahatship after emerging from one or another of the four immaterial attainments and the one who attains it after emerging from cessation. The subcommentary explains that if one obtains even a single immaterial attainment one can be called a gainer of the eight emancipations and thus be liberated in both ways. But nothing less than that will do. The exegetical texts, arguing down an unorthodox opinion that the fourth jhāna is sufficient, emphasize that only the immaterial attainments give the complete experiential liberation from material form needed to qualify for the title.

Though it is clear from this that the "one liberated in both ways" admits of grades, in the Mahānidāna Sutta the Buddha explains this type by way of the highest grade. He shows the liberated one at the height of his powers as a bhikkhu who enjoys complete proficiency in all eight emancipations and who, through the destruction of the cankers, dwells in the fruition of attainment of arahatship. By his twofold liberation he is the perfect living embodiment of the ending of the round. Since he can ascend at will through all the emancipations to enter and dwell in the cessation of perception and feeling, he is able to realize in this very life freedom from the vortex of consciousness and mentality-materiality. And since, with the attainment of arahatship, he has abolished all defilements, he is assured that with the end of his bodily existence the vortex will never turn for him again. Thus the Buddha concludes the "Great Discourse on Causation" with words that both extol the doubly liberated arahat for his own achievement and commend him as a model for others: "There is no other liberation in both ways higher or more sublime than this one."

freedom from the whirling consciousness
+ mentality & materiality

TABLE 1

THE STANDARD AND MAHĀNIDĀNA VERSIONS OF DPT. ARISING

Standard Version	**Mahānidāna Version**	
Ignorance	———	**Secondary sequence**
↓		
Volitional formations	———	
↓		Craving
Consciousness	Consciousness	↓
↓	↓ ↑	Pursuit
Mentality-materiality	Mentality-materiality	↓
		Gain
↓	↓	↓
Six sense bases	———	Decision-making
↓	↓	↓
Contact	Contact	Desire and lust
↓	↓	↓
Feeling	Feeling	Attachment
↓	↓	↓
Craving	Craving	Possessiveness
↓	↓	↓
Clinging	Clinging	Stinginess
↓	↓	↓
Existence	Existence	Safeguarding
↓	↓	↓
Birth	Birth	Various evil phenomena
↓	↓	
Aging and death	Aging and death	

Note: An arrow represents a relationship of conditionality from the condition to the dependently arisen phenomenon.

PART ONE

THE MAHĀNIDĀNA SUTTA

Dependent Arising

1. [55] Thus have I heard. On one occasion the Exalted One was living among the Kurus, where there was a town of the Kurus named Kammāsadhamma. Then the Venerable Ānanda approached the Exalted One, paid homage to him, and sat down to one side. Seated, he said to the Exalted One:

"It is wonderful and marvellous, venerable sir, how this dependent arising is so deep and appears so deep, yet to myself it seems as clear as clear can be."

"Do not say so, Ānanda! Do not say so, Ānanda! This dependent arising, Ānanda, is deep and it appears deep. Because of not understanding and not penetrating this Dhamma, Ānanda, this generation has become like a tangled skein, like a knotted ball of thread, like matted rushes and reeds, and does not pass beyond saṁsāra with its plane of misery, unfortunate destinations, and lower realms.

2. "Ānanda, if one is asked: 'Are aging and death due to a specific condition?' one should say: 'They are.' If one is asked: 'Through what condition is there aging and death?' one should say: 'With birth as condition there is aging and death.'

"Ānanda, if one is asked: 'Is birth due to a specific condition?' [56] one should say: 'It is.' If one is asked: 'Through what condition is there birth?' one should say: 'With existence as condition there is birth.'

"Ānanda, if one is asked: 'Is existence due to a specific condition?' one should say: 'It is.' If one is asked: 'Through what condition is there existence?' one should say: 'With clinging as condition there is existence.'

"Ānanda, if one is asked: 'Is clinging due to a specific condition?' one should say: 'It is.' If one is asked: 'Through what condition is there clinging?' one should say: 'With craving as condition there is clinging.'

"Ānanda, if one is asked: 'Is craving due to a specific condition?' one should say: 'It is.' If one is asked: 'Through what condition is there craving?' one should say: 'With feeling as condition there is craving.'

"Ānanda, if one is asked: 'Is feeling due to a specific condition?' one should say: 'It is.' If one is asked: 'Through what condition is there feeling?' one should say: 'With contact as condition there is feeling.'

"Ānanda, if one is asked: 'Is contact due to a specific condition?' one should say: 'It is.' If one is asked: 'Through what condition is there contact?' one should say: 'With mentality-materiality as condition there is contact.'

"Ānanda, if one is asked: 'Is mentality-materiality due to a specific condition?' one should say: 'It is.' If one is asked: 'Through what condition is there mentality-materiality?' one should say: 'With consciousness as condition there is mentality-materiality.'

"Ānanda, if one is asked: 'Is consciousness due to a specific condition?' one should say: 'It is.' If one is asked: 'Through what condition is there consciousness?' one should say: 'With mentality-materiality as condition there is consciousness.'

3. "Thus, Ānanda, with mentality-materiality as condition there is consciousness; with consciousness as condition there is mentality-materiality; with mentality-materiality as condition there is contact; with contact as condition there is feeling; with feeling as condition there is craving; with craving as condition there is clinging; with clinging as condition there is existence; with existence as condition there is birth; and with birth as condition, aging and death, sorrow, [57] lamentation, pain, grief, and despair come to be. Such is the origin of this entire mass of suffering.

Aging and Death

4. "It was said: 'With birth as condition there is aging and death.' How that is so, Ānanda, should be understood in this way: If there were absolutely and utterly no birth of any kind anywhere—that is, of gods into the state of gods, of celestials into the state of celestials, of spirits, demons, human beings, quadrupeds, winged creatures, and reptiles, each into their own state—if there were no birth of beings of any sort into any state, then, in the complete absence of birth, with the cessation of birth, would aging and death be discerned?"

"Certainly not, venerable sir."

"Therefore, Ānanda, this is the cause, source, origin, and condition for aging and death, namely, birth.

Birth

5. "It was said: 'With existence as condition there is birth.' How that is so, Ānanda, should be understood in this way: If there were absolutely and utterly no existence of any kind anywhere—that is, no sense-sphere existence, fine-material existence, or immaterial existence—then, in the complete absence of existence, with the cessation of existence, would birth be discerned?"

"Certainly not, venerable sir."

"Therefore, Ānanda, this is the cause, source, origin, and condition for birth, namely, existence.

Existence

6. "It was said: 'With clinging as condition there is existence.' How that is so, Ānanda, should be understood in this way: If there were absolutely and utterly no clinging of any kind [58] anywhere—that is, no clinging to sense pleasures, clinging to views, clinging to precepts and observances, or clinging to a doctrine of self—then, in the complete absence of clinging, with the cessation of clinging, would existence be discerned?"

"Certainly not, venerable sir."

"Therefore, Ānanda, this is the cause, source, origin, and condition for existence, namely, clinging.

Clinging

7. "It was said: 'With craving as condition there is clinging.' How that is so, Ānanda, should be understood in this way: If there were absolutely and utterly no craving of any kind anywhere—that is, no craving for visible forms, craving for sounds, craving for smells, craving for tastes, craving for tangibles, or craving for mental objects—then, in the complete absence of craving, with the cessation of craving, would clinging be discerned?"

"Certainly not, venerable sir."

"Therefore, Ānanda, this is the cause, source, origin, and condition for clinging, namely, craving.

Craving

8. "It was said: 'With feeling as condition there is craving.' How that is so, Ānanda, should be understood in this way: If there were absolutely and utterly no feeling of any kind anywhere—that is, no feeling born of eye-contact, feeling born of ear-contact, feeling born of

nose-contact, feeling born of tongue-contact, feeling born of body-contact, or feeling born of mind-contact—then, in the complete absence of feeling, with the cessation of feeling, would craving be discerned?"

"Certainly not, venerable sir."

"Therefore, Ānanda, this is the cause, source, origin, and condition for craving, namely, feeling.

Dependent on Craving

9. "Thus, Ānanda, in dependence upon feeling there is craving; in dependence upon craving there is pursuit; in dependence upon pursuit there is gain; in dependence upon gain there is decision-making; in dependence upon decision-making there is desire and lust; in dependence upon desire and lust there is attachment; in dependence upon attachment there is possessiveness; in dependence upon possessiveness there is stinginess; [59] in dependence upon stinginess there is safeguarding; and because of safeguarding, various evil unwholesome phenomena originate—the taking up of clubs and weapons, conflicts, quarrels, and disputes, insulting speech, slander, and falsehoods.

10. "It was said: 'Because of safeguarding, various evil unwholesome phenomena originate—the taking up of clubs and weapons, conflicts, quarrels, and disputes, insulting speech, slander, and falsehoods.' How that is so, Ānanda, should be understood in this way: If there were absolutely and utterly no safeguarding of any kind anywhere, then, in the complete absence of safeguarding, with the cessation of safeguarding, would those various evil unwholesome phenomena originate?"

"Certainly not, venerable sir."

"Therefore, Ānanda, this is the cause, source, origin, and condition for those various evil unwholesome phenomena, namely, safeguarding.

11. "It was said: 'In dependence upon stinginess there is safeguarding.' How that is so, Ānanda, should be understood in this way: If there were absolutely and utterly no stinginess of any kind anywhere, then, in the complete absence of stinginess, with the cessation of stinginess, would safeguarding be discerned?"

"Certainly not, venerable sir."

"Therefore, Ānanda, this is the cause, source, origin, and condition for safeguarding, namely, stinginess.

12. "It was said: 'In dependence upon possessiveness there is stinginess.' How that is so, Ānanda, should be understood in this way: [60] If there were absolutely and utterly no possessiveness of any kind anywhere, then, in the complete absence of possessiveness, with the cessation of possessiveness, would stinginess be discerned?"

"Certainly not, venerable sir."

"Therefore, Ānanda, this is the cause, source, origin, and condition for stinginess, namely, possessiveness.

13. "It was said: 'In dependence upon attachment there is possessiveness.' How that is so, Ānanda, should be understood in this way: If there were absolutely and utterly no attachment of any kind anywhere, then, in the complete absence of attachment, with the cessation of attachment, would possessiveness be discerned?"

"Certainly not, venerable sir."

"Therefore, Ānanda, this is the cause, source, origin, and condition for possessiveness, namely, attachment.

14. "It was said: 'In dependence upon desire and lust there is attachment.' How that is so, Ānanda, should be understood in this way: If there were absolutely and utterly no desire and lust of any kind anywhere, then, in the complete absence of desire and lust, with the cessation of desire and lust, would attachment be discerned?"

"Certainly not, venerable sir."

"Therefore, Ānanda, this is the cause, source, origin, and condition for attachment, namely, desire and lust.

15. "It was said: 'In dependence upon decision-making there is desire and lust.' How that is so, Ānanda, should be understood in this way: If there were absolutely and utterly no decision-making of any kind anywhere, then, in the complete absence of decision-making, with the cessation of decision-making, would desire and lust be discerned?" [61]

"Certainly not, venerable sir."

"Therefore, Ānanda, this is the cause, source, origin, and condition for desire and lust, namely, decision-making.

16. "It was said: 'In dependence upon gain there is decision-making.' How that is so, Ānanda, should be understood in this way: If there were absolutely and utterly no gain of any kind anywhere, then, in the complete absence of gain, with the cessation of gain, would decision-making be discerned?"

"Certainly not, venerable sir."

"Therefore, Ānanda, this is the cause, source, origin, and condition for decision-making, namely, gain.

17. "It was said: 'In dependence upon pursuit there is gain.' How that is so, Ānanda, should be understood in this way: If there were absolutely and utterly no pursuit of any kind anywhere, then, in the complete absence of pursuit, with the cessation of pursuit, would gain be discerned?"

"Certainly not, venerable sir."

"Therefore, Ānanda, this is the cause, source, origin, and condition for gain, namely, pursuit.

18. "It was said: 'In dependence upon craving there is pursuit.' How that is so, Ānanda, should be understood in this way: If there were absolutely and utterly no craving of any kind anywhere—that is, no craving for sense pleasures, craving for existence, or craving for non-existence—then, in the complete absence of craving, with the cessation of craving, would pursuit be discerned?"

"Certainly not, venerable sir."

"Therefore, Ānanda, this is the cause, source, origin, and condition for pursuit, namely, craving.

"Thus, Ānanda, these two phenomena, being a duality, converge into a unity in feeling. [62]

Feeling

19. "It was said: 'With contact as condition there is feeling.' How that is so, Ānanda, should be understood in this way: If there were absolutely and utterly no contact of any kind anywhere—that is, no eye-contact, ear-contact, nose-contact, tongue-contact, body-contact, or mind-contact—then, in the complete absence of contact, with the cessation of contact, would feeling be discerned?"

"Certainly not, venerable sir."

"Therefore, Ānanda, this is the cause, source, origin, and condition for feeling, namely, contact.

Contact

20. "It was said: 'With mentality-materiality as condition there is contact.' How that is so, Ānanda, should be understood in this way: If those qualities, traits, signs, and indicators through which there is a description of the mental body were all absent, would designation-contact be discerned in the material body?"

"Certainly not, venerable sir."

"If those qualities, traits, signs, and indicators through which there is a description of the material body were all absent, would impingement-contact be discerned in the mental body?"

"Certainly not, venerable sir."

"If those qualities, traits, signs, and indicators through which there is a description of the mental body and the material body were all absent, would either designation-contact or impingement-contact be discerned?"

"Certainly not, venerable sir."

"If those qualities, traits, signs, and indicators through which there is a description of mentality-materiality were all absent, would contact be discerned?"

"Certainly not, venerable sir."

"Therefore, Ānanda, this is the cause, source, origin, and condition for contact, namely, mentality-materiality.

Mentality-Materiality

21. "It was said: 'With consciousness as condition there is mentality-materiality.' [63] How that is so, Ānanda, should be understood in this way: If consciousness were not to descend into the mother's womb, would mentality-materiality take shape in the womb?"

"Certainly not, venerable sir."

"If, after descending into the womb, consciousness were to depart, would mentality-materiality be generated into this present state of being?"

"Certainly not, venerable sir."

"If the consciousness of a young boy or girl were to be cut off, would mentality-materiality grow up, develop, and reach maturity?"

"Certainly not, venerable sir."

"Therefore, Ānanda, this is the cause, source, origin, and condition for mentality-materiality, namely, consciousness.

Consciousness

22. "It was said: 'With mentality-materiality as condition there is consciousness.' How that is so, Ānanda, should be understood in this way: If consciousness were not to gain a footing in mentality-materiality, would an origination of the mass of suffering—of future birth, aging, and death—be discerned?"

"Certainly not, venerable sir."

"Therefore, Ānanda, this is the cause, source, origin, and condition for consciousness, namely, mentality-materiality.

"It is to this extent, Ānanda, that one can be born, age, and die, pass away and re-arise, to this extent that there is a pathway for designation, to this extent that there is a pathway for language, to this extent that there is a pathway for description, to this extent that there is a sphere for wisdom, to this extent that the round turns [64] for describing this state of being, that is, when there is mentality-materiality together with consciousness.[1]

Descriptions of Self

23. "In what ways, Ānanda, does one describing self describe it? Describing self as having material form and as limited, one describes it thus: 'My self has material form and is limited.' Or describing self as having material form and as infinite, one describes it thus: 'My self has material form and is infinite.' Or describing self as immaterial and limited, one describes it thus: 'My self is immaterial and limited.' Or describing self as immaterial and infinite, one describes it thus: 'My self is immaterial and infinite.'

24. "Therein, Ānanda, one who describes self as having material form and as limited either describes such a self (as existing only) in the present or he describes such a self (as existing) there in the future, or he thinks: 'That which is not thus, I will convert towards the state of being thus.'[2] This being so, it can aptly be said that a settled view (of self) as having material form and as limited underlies this.

"One who describes self as having material form and as infinite either describes such a self ... (*as above*) ... This being so, it can aptly be said that a settled view (of self) as having material form and as infinite underlies this.

"One who describes self as immaterial and limited either describes such a self ... (*as above*) ... This being so, it can aptly be said that a settled view (of self) as immaterial and limited underlies this.

"One who describes self as immaterial and infinite either describes such a self ... (*as above*) ... [65] This being so, it can aptly be said that a settled view (of self) as immaterial and infinite underlies this.

"It is in these ways, Ānanda, that one describing self describes it.

Non-Descriptions of Self

25. "In what ways, Ānanda, does one not describing self not describe it? Not describing self as having material form and as limited, one does not describe it thus: 'My self has material form and is limited.' Or not describing self as having material form and as infinite, one does not describe it thus: 'My self has material form and is infinite.' Or not describing self as immaterial and limited, one does not describe it thus: 'My self is immaterial and limited.' Or not describing self as immaterial and infinite, one does not describe it thus: 'My self is immaterial and infinite.'

26. "Therein, Ānanda, one who does not describe self as having material form and as limited does not describe such a self (as existing only) in the present, nor does he describe such a self (as existing) there

in the future, nor does he think: 'That which is not thus, I will convert towards the state of being thus.' This being so, it can aptly be said that a settled view (of self) as having material form and as limited does not underlie this.

"One who does not describe self as having material form and as infinite does not describe such a self … (*as above*) … This being so, it can aptly be said that a settled view (of self) as having material form and as infinite does not underlie this.

"One who does not describe self as immaterial and limited does not describe such a self … (*as above*) … This being so, it can aptly be said that a settled view (of self) as immaterial and limited does not underlie this.

"One who describes self as immaterial and infinite does not describe such a self … (*as above*) … [66] This being so, it can aptly be said that a settled view (of self) as immaterial and infinite does not underlie this.

"It is in these ways, Ānanda, that one not describing self does not describe it.

Considerations of Self

27. "In what ways, Ānanda, does one considering (the idea of) self consider it? One considering (the idea of) self either considers feeling as self, saying: 'Feeling is my self.' Or he considers: 'Feeling is not my self; my self is without experience of feeling.' Or he considers: 'Feeling is not my self, but my self is not without experience of feeling. My self feels; for my self is subject to feeling.'

28. "Therein, Ānanda, the one who says 'Feeling is my self' should be asked: 'Friend, there are these three kinds of feeling—pleasant feeling, painful feeling, and neither-painful-nor-pleasant feeling. Of these three kinds of feeling, which do you consider as self?'

"Ānanda, on the occasion when one experiences a pleasant feeling one does not, on that same occasion, experience a painful feeling or a neither-painful-nor-pleasant feeling; on that occasion one experiences only a pleasant feeling. On the occasion when one experiences a painful feeling one does not, on that same occasion, experience a pleasant feeling or a neither-painful-nor-pleasant feeling; on that occasion one experiences only a painful feeling. On the occasion when one experiences a neither-painful-nor-pleasant feeling one does not, on that same occasion, experience a pleasant feeling or a painful feeling; on that occasion one experiences only a neither-painful-nor-pleasant feeling.

29. "Ānanda, pleasant feeling is impermanent, conditioned, depend-

ently arisen, subject to destruction, falling away, fading out, and ceasing. Painful feeling [67] is impermanent, conditioned, dependently arisen, subject to destruction, falling away, fading out, and ceasing. Neither-painful-nor-pleasant feeling is impermanent, conditioned, dependently arisen, subject to destruction, falling away, fading out, and ceasing.

"If, when experiencing a pleasant feeling, one thinks: 'This is my self,' then with the ceasing of that pleasant feeling one thinks: 'My self has disappeared.' If, when experiencing a painful feeling, one thinks: 'This is my self,' then with the ceasing of that painful feeling one thinks: 'My self has disappeared.' If, when experiencing a neither-painful-nor-pleasant feeling, one thinks: 'This is my self,' then with the ceasing of that neither-painful-nor-pleasant feeling one thinks: 'My self has disappeared.'

"Thus one who says 'Feeling is my self' considers as self something which, even here and now, is impermanent, a mixture of pleasure and pain, and subject to arising and falling away. Therefore, Ānanda, because of this it is not acceptable to consider: 'Feeling is my self.'

30. "Ānanda, the one who says 'Feeling is not my self; my self is without experience of feeling'—he should be asked: 'Friend, where there is nothing at all that is felt, could the idea "I am"[3] occur there?'."

"Certainly not, venerable sir."

"Therefore, Ānanda, because of this it is not acceptable to consider: 'Feeling is not my self; my self is without experience of feeling.'

31. "Ānanda, the one who says 'Feeling is not my self, but my self is not without experience of feeling. My self feels; for my self is subject to feeling'—he should be asked: 'Friend, if feeling were to cease absolutely and utterly without remainder, then, in the complete absence of feeling, with the cessation of feeling, could (the idea) "I am this" occur there?'."

"Certainly not, venerable sir."

"Therefore, Ānanda, because of this it is not acceptable to consider: [68] 'Feeling is not my self, but my self is not without experience of feeling. My self feels; for my self is subject to feeling.'

32. "Ānanda, when a bhikkhu does not consider feeling as self, and does not consider self as without experience of feeling, and does not consider: 'My self feels; for my self is subject to feeling'—then, being without such considerations, he does not cling to anything in the world. Not clinging, he is not agitated. Not being agitated, he personally attains nibbāna. He understands: 'Destroyed is birth, the holy life has been lived, what had to be done has been done, there is no returning to this state of being.'

"Ānanda, if anyone should say of a bhikkhu whose mind has been thus liberated, that he holds the view 'A Tathāgata exists after death'—that would not be proper; or that he holds the view 'A Tathāgata does not exist after death'—that would not be proper; or that he holds the view 'A Tathāgata both exists and does not exist after death'—that would not be proper; or that he holds the view 'A Tathāgata neither exists nor does not exist after death'—that would not be proper. For what reason? Because that bhikkhu is liberated by directly knowing this: the extent of designation and the extent of the pathway for designation, the extent of language and the extent of the pathway for language, the extent of description and the extent of the pathway for description, the extent of wisdom and the extent of the sphere for wisdom, the extent of the round and the extent to which the round turns. To say of a bhikkhu who is liberated by directly knowing this that he holds the view 'One does not know and does not see'—that would not be proper.

The Seven Stations for Consciousness

33. "Ānanda, there are these seven stations for consciousness and two bases. What are the seven?

"There are, Ānanda, beings who are diverse in body [69] and diverse in perception, such as human beings, some gods, and some beings in the lower realms. This is the first station for consciousness.

"There are beings who are diverse in body but identical in perception, such as the gods of the Brahma-order who are generated through the first (jhāna). This is the second station for consciousness.

"There are beings who are identical in body but diverse in perception, such as the gods of streaming radiance. This is the third station for consciousness.

"There are beings who are identical in body and identical in perception, such as the gods of refulgent beauty. This is the fourth station for consciousness.

"There are beings who, through the complete surmounting of perceptions of material form, the passing away of perceptions of impingement, and non-attention to perceptions of diversity, (contemplating) 'Space is infinite,' arrive at the base of the infinity of space. This is the fifth station for consciousness.

"There are beings who, having completely surmounted the base of the infinity of space, (contemplating) 'Consciousness is infinite,' arrive at the base of the infinity of consciousness. This is the sixth station for consciousness.

"There are beings who, having completely surmounted the base of the infinity of consciousness, (contemplating) 'There is nothing,' arrive at the base of nothingness. This is the seventh station for consciousness.

"The base of non-percipient beings and, second, the base of neither perception nor non-perception—(these are the two bases).

34. "Therein, Ānanda, if one understands the first station for consciousness, that of beings who are diverse in body and diverse in perception, and if one understands its origin, its passing away, its satisfaction, its unsatisfactoriness, and the escape from it, is it proper for one to seek enjoyment in it?" [70]

"Certainly not, venerable sir."

"If one understands the remaining stations for consciousness ... the base of non-percipient beings ... the base of neither perception nor non-perception, and if one understands its origin, its passing away, its satisfaction, its unsatisfactoriness, and the escape from it, is it proper for one to seek enjoyment in it?"

"Certainly not, venerable sir."

"Ānanda, when a bhikkhu—having understood as they really are the origin, passing away, satisfaction, unsatisfactoriness, and escape in regard to these seven stations for consciousness and two bases—is liberated through non-clinging, then he is called a bhikkhu liberated by wisdom.

The Eight Emancipations

35. "Ānanda, there are these eight emancipations. What are the eight?

"One possessing material form sees material forms. This is the first emancipation.

"One not perceiving material forms internally sees material forms externally. This is the second emancipation. [71]

"One is released upon the idea of the beautiful. This is the third emancipation.

"Through the complete surmounting of perceptions of material form, the passing away of perceptions of impingement, and non-attention to perceptions of diversity, (contemplating) 'Space is infinite,' one enters and dwells in the base of the infinity of space. This is the fourth emancipation.

"Having completely surmounted the base of the infinity of space, (contemplating) 'Consciousness is infinite,' one enters and dwells in the base of the infinity of consciousness. This is the fifth emancipation.

"Having completely surmounted the base of the infinity of consciousness, (contemplating) 'There is nothing,' one enters and dwells in the base of nothingness. This is the sixth emancipation.

"Having completely surmounted the base of nothingness, one enters and dwells in the base of neither perception nor non-perception. This is the seventh emancipation.

"Having completely surmounted the base of neither perception nor non-perception, one enters and dwells in the cessation of perception and feeling. This is the eighth emancipation.

36. "Ānanda, when a bhikkhu attains these eight emancipations in forward order, in reverse order, and in both forward order and reverse order; when he attains them and emerges from them wherever he wants, in whatever way he wants, and for as long as he wants, and when, through the destruction of the cankers, he here and now enters and dwells in the cankerless liberation of mind, liberation by wisdom, having realized it for himself with direct knowledge, then he is called a bhikkhu who is liberated in both ways. And, Ānanda, there is no other liberation in both ways higher or more sublime than this one."

Thus spoke the Exalted One. The Venerable Ānanda, being pleased, rejoiced in the Exalted One's words.

PART TWO

THE COMMENTARIAL EXEGESIS OF THE MAHĀNIDĀNA SUTTA

1. Introductory Section

1. THEN THE VENERABLE ĀNANDA APPROACHED THE EXALTED ONE …

CY. [484] At what time, and for what reason, did the Venerable Ānanda approach the Exalted One? He approached in the evening, for the purpose of asking a question about the principle of conditionality. It is said that on that day the Venerable Ānanda, in order to benefit families, walked for alms in the village of Kammāsadhamma, (going along) as if depositing a bundle of a thousand gold pieces at the door of each house [because, by accepting their almsfood, he enabled them to generate a great mass of merit]. When he returned from his almsround he did his duties to the Teacher. When the Teacher entered the Fragrant Cottage, he venerated him, went to his own day-quarters, and did his duties to his own pupils. After they departed, he swept his quarters, prepared his leather mat, cooled off his hands and feet with water from the waterpot, and sitting down cross-legged, he attained to the attainment of the fruit of stream-entry. Emerging from the attainment at the predetermined time, he immersed his mind in the principle of conditionality. He explored the twelve-factored principle of conditionality three times, first starting from the beginning thus: "With ignorance as condition volitional formations come to be," and working down to the end, then working from the end back to the beginning, and then working from both ends to the middle and from the middle to both ends. As he explored it, the principle of conditionality [485] became transparent to him and it appeared "as clear as clear can be."

Thereupon he considered: "The Buddhas all say that the principle of conditionality is deep and appears deep; yet to myself, a disciple with limited knowledge, it appears clear, transparent, and evident. Does it appear so only to myself or to others as well?" Then he thought: "Let me take this question to the Exalted One. For surely the Exalted One will treat this question of mine as an opportunity for teaching and, as if lifting up Mount Sineru along with its surroundings, he will elucidate the matter by explaining a discourse. For there are four areas where the thundering of the Buddhas becomes great, their knowledge enters its proper field, the greatness of the Buddha-knowledge is discerned, and their teaching becomes deep, stamped with the three characteristics, connected with emptiness, namely, the promulgation of the Vinaya, the classification of the diversity of planes, the exposition of the principle of conditionality, and the classification of the diversity of tenets."[1]

Though the Venerable Ānanda ordinarily approached the Exalted One a hundred or a thousand times a day, he never approached without a cause or reason. So that day he rose up from his day-quarters, shook out his leather mat and, taking it along, in the evening he approached the Buddha with his question in mind, thinking: "I will confront the elephant-like Buddha and hear his trumpeting cry of knowledge. I will confront the lion-like Buddha and hear his lion's roar of knowledge. I will confront the stallion-like Buddha and see his stride of knowledge." Thus it was said above: "He approached in the evening, for the purpose of asking a question about the principle of conditionality."

SUB. CY. "As if lifting up Mount Sineru along with its surroundings": by this phrase he expresses the great difficulty of expounding such a teaching. "The thundering of the Buddhas becomes great": this passage is undertaken to show that just as the understanding of the promulgation of the Vinaya, the diversity of planes, and the diversity of tenets is the domain only of the omniscient knowledge, not shared by others, so too is the analysis of conditionality, which is free from the two extremes and devoid of an independent agent and experiencer.[2]

"Their thundering becomes great": the thundering of their teaching, occurring with diverse methods, becomes great, vast, and many-faceted because of the complexity and difficulty of the subject to be taught.

"Their knowledge enters its proper sphere": hence their knowledge of how to teach repeatedly enters into the phenomena to be taught, laying bare their divisions.

"The greatness of the Buddha-knowledge is discerned": in the teaching and penetration of such a Dhamma, the loftiness of the Buddha's knowledge of how to teach and his knowledge of penetration becomes evident.

Herein, the canonical statement "All the Exalted Buddha's verbal action is preceded and accompanied by knowledge" (M.Nd., p. 178) establishes that the Exalted One's teaching is never devoid of knowledge and always occurs like a lion's roar. Nevertheless, because of the subject to be taught, this present teaching can be considered deeper than the others and the sphere to be distinctively entered upon by his knowledge.

THIS DEPENDENT ARISING IS SO DEEP AND APPEARS SO DEEP ...

CY. Being deep, it appears deep. For something (a body of water) might be shallow yet appear deep, like stagnant water having a dark colour because of rotting leaves, etc.; this might be only knee-deep, yet appear to be a hundred fathoms.[3] Another body of water might be deep yet appear shallow, like the serene water of the Jewel River, which is a hundred fathoms deep yet seems to be knee-deep. Other water might be shallow and appear shallow, like the water in a pot, etc. And still other water [486] might be deep and appear deep, like the water in the ocean at the foot of Mount Sineru. Thus water can be described in four ways.

But this is not so in regard to dependent arising. This can be described in only one way: "it is deep and appears deep." But though this is so, the Venerable Ānanda says: "To myself it seems as clear as clear can be. How wonderful and marvellous, venerable sir!" Thus revealing his own astonishment, he asked a question, sat down, and became silent.

SUB. CY. *Query*: Isn't it true that dependent arising is exclusively deep? Then why is its deep appearance mentioned?

Reply: It is mentioned to show that it is exclusively deep. To show by way of contrast that it is exclusively deep, the commentator describes four alternatives that apply to something else and then shows that, of the four, only the last is applicable to dependent arising.

DO NOT SAY SO, ĀNANDA!

CY. Hearing his statement, the Exalted One thought to himself: "Ānanda says that a matter which belongs to the domain of the Buddhas is clear to himself. This is like stretching out one's hand to take hold of the highest plane of existence, like trying to cut through Mount Sineru and remove its core, like wanting to cross the ocean without a ship, or like turning over the earth and trying to take its nutritive essence. Let me point out its depth to him." Then he said: "Do not say so, Ānanda!"

SUB. CY. By means of four similes the commentator illustrates those deep qualities on account of which dependent arising is called "deep." Just as it is not possible to stretch out one's hand and take hold of the highest plane of existence because of its distance, so it is not possible for one with ordinary knowledge to grasp the meaning of the volitional formations being originated and sustained with ignorance as condition, etc. Just as it is not possible for an ordinary person to break open Mount Sineru and remove its core, so it is not possible for one with ordinary knowledge to penetratively understand, through division and analysis, the phenomena and meanings involved in dependent arising. Just as it is not possible for an ordinary person to cross the ocean by the strength of his arms, so it is not possible for one with ordinary knowledge to cross dependent arising by way of teaching it. And just as it is not possible for an ordinary person to turn over the earth and take its nutritive essence, so it is not possible for one with ordinary knowledge to uncover and grasp the conditioning nature of the conditions thus: "In such and such ways ignorance, etc., is a condition for volitional formations, etc." Thus the four similes can be interpreted by way of the fourfold depth of dependent arising.[4]

This interpretation of the meaning is made by way of ordinary knowledge, since all those who have seen the truths[5] possess penetration (of dependent arising). Nevertheless, because disciples and paccekabuddhas have only limited knowledge of it while Buddhas alone have unlimited knowledge, dependent arising is called "a matter which belongs to the domain of the Buddhas."

2. The Extolling of Ānanda

CY. The Exalted One says "Do not say so, Ānanda!" both to extol the Venerable Ānanda and to restrain him. Extolling him, he implies: "Ānanda, you have great wisdom and lucid knowledge. Thus dependent arising, though deep, seems clear to you. But for others it cannot be characterized as clear; rather, it is deep and it appears deep."

Four similes are given to illustrate this. A well-trained champion wrestler, it is said, who had been nourished with nutritious food for six months and had exercised with a wrestler's stone,[6] was going to the fighting arena during a carnival when they showed him a wrestler's stone along the way. He asked: "What is that?" – "A wrestler's stone." – "Bring it here." – "We cannot lift it," they said. Then he went over to it himself. Saying "What is so heavy with this?" he lifted two such stones with two hands, threw them away like balls, and continued on his way. Though the stone was light for the wrestler, it could not be called light for the others. As the wrestler had been nourished with nutritious food for six months, so the Venerable Ānanda had been endowed with the aspiration (to become a Buddha's personal attendant) for 100,000 aeons. As for the wrestler with his great strength the stone was light, but not for others, so for the Elder Ānanda [487] with his great wisdom dependent arising was clear, but it could not be called clear for others.

In the ocean there is a fish called the Timirapingala, 500 yojanas long.[7] When it shakes its right fin, it is said, it stirs up the water in an area of 500 yojanas; similarly for its left fin, its tail, and its head. But when it plays about in the water—shaking both fins, striking the water with its tail, ducking its head in and out—it churns up the water in an area of 700 or 800 yojanas until it becomes just like water boiling in a pot on the stove. Even water in a region 300 yojanas deep cannot cover its back. This fish might say: "They are always saying that the ocean is deep. How can it be deep? I can't even find enough water to cover my back." For the Timirapingala, with its vast body, the ocean might be shallow, but it cannot be called shallow for the smaller fish. Similarly, for the Elder Ānanda, with his vast knowledge, dependent arising might be clear, but it cannot be called clear for others.

The royal Supaṇṇa bird is 250 yojanas long, his right and left wings fifty yojanas, his tail sixty yojanas, his neck thirty yojanas, his beak nine yojanas, and his feet twelve yojanas. When he starts to stir up a wind even an area 700 or 800 yojanas is not enough. He might say: "They are always saying that space is infinite. How can it be infinite? I can't even find enough room to stretch out my wings and stir up a wind." For the royal Supaṇṇa bird, with his vast body, space might be limited, but it cannot be called limited for smaller birds. Similarly for the Elder Ānanda with his vast knowledge.

Rāhu, the lord of the titans, is 4,800 yojanas tall. His armspan is 1,200 yojanas, [488] his body 600 yojanas thick, his palms and soles 300 yojanas, so too his mouth. Each segment of his fingers is fifty yojanas, as is the distance between his eyebrows. His brow is 300 yojanas and his head 900 yojanas. When he enters the ocean the deepest water comes only up to his knees. He might say: "They are always saying that the ocean is deep. How can it be deep? I can't even find water deep enough to cover my knees." For Rāhu, with his vast body, the ocean might be shallow, but it cannot be called shallow for others. Similarly for the Elder Ānanda with his vast knowledge.

Dependent arising, though deep, appeared clear to the Elder Ānanda for four reasons: (1) because he was endowed with decisive supporting conditions from the past; (2) because of his diligence in study; (3) because he was a stream-enterer; and (4) because he was highly learned.[8]

(1) The Venerable Ānanda's endowment with decisive supporting conditions from the past began when he formed his original aspiration to become the personal attendant of a Buddha. This took place 100,000 aeons ago, during the period when the Buddha Padumuttara was living in the world. At that time Ānanda was the Buddha's younger half-brother, a prince named Sumana. On one occasion he supported the Buddha Padumuttara and a Sangha of 100,000 bhikkhus during the annual three months' rains residence. At the end of this period he offered food and robes to the Buddha and the Sangha, and dedicated the merit he acquired by his good deeds to becoming the personal attendant of a future Buddha. The Buddha Padumuttara then foretold that his aspiration would come to fulfilment after 100,000 aeons, in the dispensation of the Buddha Gotama. Following this, he continued to perform meritorious deeds through the succeeding lifetimes until, in the present life, he went forth under the Buddha Gotama and became established in the fruit of stream-entry. Thus the Venerable Ānanda was endowed with decisive supporting conditions from the past, and because he was so endowed, dependent arising, though deep, appeared clear to him.[9] [488-492]

(2) "Diligence in study" refers to repeatedly studying [the texts] under revered teachers, listening [to explanations of their meaning], questioning [about knotty points], and retaining in mind [the texts and their meaning]. The Elder Ānanda had done that exceedingly well. For this reason too dependent arising, though deep, appeared clear to him.

(3) Further, the principle of conditionality appears clear to stream-enterers and the Venerable Ānanda was a stream-enterer.

(4) For those who are highly learned, the delimitation of mentality-materiality becomes as evident as a bed and chair in a small room illuminated by a lamp, [493] and the Venerable Ānanda was the chief of those who are highly learned. Because of his great learning dependent arising, though deep, appeared clear to him.

SUB. CY. The principle of conditionality appears clear to stream-enterers because, with the dispelling of delusion, the principle "whatever is subject to arising is all subject to ceasing"[10] presents itself to them by way of personal direct cognition.

The "delimitation of mentality-materiality" is comprehension by delimiting mentality-materiality together with its conditions.

3. The Depth of Dependent Arising

CY. Dependent arising is deep in four respects: (1) because of its depth of meaning; (2) because of its depth of phenomena; (3) because of its depth of teaching; and (4) because of its depth of penetration.[11]

(1) Its depth of meaning (should be understood as) the deep meaning of aging and death being originated and sustained with birth as condition ... the deep meaning of volitional formations being originated and sustained with ignorance as condition.

SUB. CY. "The meaning of aging and death being originated and sustained with birth as condition": having originated through the condition of birth, aging and death become further extended in accordance with their own concurrent condition, i.e. they continue to occur. Or else the commentary's phrase may be construed as "the meaning of originated" (*sambhūtaṭṭha*) and "the meaning of sustained" (*samudāgataṭṭha*). The meaning of aging and death being originated with birth as condition is explained thus: "There are no aging and death that do not come to be through birth, and there are none that come to be without birth, on account of something else." The meaning of aging and death being sustained with birth as condition is that aging and death become manifest in accordance with the kind of birth and with the ways it serves as a condition. This meaning is "deep" in the sense of fathomless, since it does not give a footing for knowledge to those who have not accumulated wholesome collections (of meritorious qualities). The same method of exegesis should be applied to the other terms.

CY. (2) Its depth of phenomena (should be understood as) the deep meaning of ignorance being a condition for volitional formations ... the deep meaning of birth being a condition for aging and death.

SUB. CY. "The deep meaning of ignorance being a condition for volitional formations": the mode (*ākāra*) through which, and the stage (*avatthā*) at which, ignorance becomes a condition for volitional formations, and the stage at which it does so, are difficult to comprehend. As both of these are difficult to comprehend, the meaning of ignorance being a condition for volitional formations through nine modes is "deep" in the sense of fathomless, since it does not give a footing for knowledge to those who have not accumulated wholesome collections (of meritorious qualities).[12] The same method of exegesis should be applied to the other terms.

CY. (3) Its depth of teaching (should be understood) thus. In some places in the suttas dependent arising is taught in forward order, in some in reverse order, in some in both forward and reverse order, in some beginning from the middle in forward order, or in reverse order, or in both. In some places three connections and four groups are taught, in some two connections and three groups, in some one connection and two groups.[13]

SUB. CY. Here "forward order" (*anuloma*) means: through the arising of the condition the conditionally arisen phenomenon arises. "Reverse order" (*paṭiloma*) means: through the cessation of the condition the conditionally arisen phenomenon ceases. But forward order also means starting from the beginning and going through to the end; reverse order, starting from the end and going back to the beginning.

In a teaching that proceeds in forward order from the beginning or in reverse order from the end, there are three connections and four groups. In a teaching that starts from the middle and goes back in reverse order—such as the passage, "Bhikkhus, what is the source for these four kinds of nutriment?" etc. (S.XII,11; ii,11)—there are two connections and three groups. So too for a teaching that starts from the middle and goes forward in direct order, such as the passage: "In dependence upon the eye and visible forms there arises eye-consciousness. The conjunction of the three is contact. With contact as condition there is feeling," etc. (S.XII,43; ii,72). In the passage: "When one lives contemplating satisfaction in phenomena which stimulate the fetters, craving increases. With craving as condition there is clinging," etc. (S.XII,53; ii,86), there is one connection and two groups. Dependent arising is even taught by way of a single factor. Such is found in the passage: "The instructed noble disciple attends to this carefully and methodically in terms of dependent arising: 'When there is this, that comes to be; with the arising of this, that arises. When this is absent, that does not come to be; with the ceasing of this, that ceases.' In dependence upon a contact to be felt as pleasant there arises a pleasant feeling," (S.XII,62; ii,96). That should be understood by way of this sutta.

Thus, because it must be presented in different ways for different reasons, dependent arising is deep in teaching. Thus the commentator says: "This is its depth of teaching." For no kind of knowledge other that the omniscient knowledge (of a Buddha) can find a footing in it.

CY. (4) Its depth of penetration (should be understood thus): Deep is the meaning of ignorance as not knowing, not seeing, and non-penetration of the truths. Deep is the meaning of volitional formations as volitionally forming, accumulating, lustfulness, and lustlessness; the meaning of consciousness as emptiness, absence of an agent, and manifestation of rebirth-linking without transmigration; the meaning of mentality-materiality as simultaneous arising, separableness, insep-

** special attention

arableness, bending, and deformation; the meaning of the six sense bases as predominants, the world, doors, fields, and possession of objective domains; the meaning of contact as contacting, striking, conjunction, and encounter; the meaning of feeling as the experiencing of the object's taste, as being either pleasant, painful, or neutral, as being soulless, and as being felt; the meaning of craving as seeking enjoyment, attachment, as being a stream, a creeper, a river, and an ocean, and as being insatiable; the meaning of clinging as taking, grasping, adherence, misapprehension, and being difficult to overcome; the meaning of existence as accumulating, volitionally forming, and throwing beings into the different modes of origin, destinations, stations, and abodes; the meaning of birth as taking birth, being born, conception, generation, and manifestation; and the meaning of aging and death as destruction, falling away, breakup, and change.

The intrinsic natures of these states such as ignorance, etc., by the penetration of which these states themselves are penetrated through their essential characteristics—those intrinsic natures are deep. In this way the depth of penetration (of dependent arising) should be understood.

SUB. CY. Ignorance has the meaning "not knowing" since it is the opposite of knowledge with its characteristic of knowing. It has the meaning "not seeing" since it is the opposite of seeing by direct cognition of the object. It has the meaning "non-penetration of the truths" since, through its own intrinsic nature, it does not allow one to penetrate the essential actuality of the truths of suffering, etc., but persistently conceals them and envelops them.

"Accumulating" is the collecting together or piling up of its associated phenomena in accordance with its own function. "Lustfulness" is one part of the demeritorious volitional formations, "lustlessness" the rest. Or else all demeritorious volitional formations, as a condition for the arising of lust, as increasing lust, and as not opposed to lust, are called "lustfulness," while the other volitional formations (meritorious and imperturbable), as the opposite of this, are called "lustlessness."

Consciousness's meaning of emptiness is deep because consciousness is said to be the distinctive basis for the misapprehension of self. As it is said: "For a long time the uninstructed worldling has been attached to this, appropriated it, and misapprehended it, thus: 'This is mine, this I am, this is my self' " (S.XII,61; ii,94). Consciousness's meanings of absence of an agent and manifestation of rebirth-linking without transmigration are deep because of the strength of people's adherence to a self as the agent of consciousness and as the subject of transmigration in saṁsāra.

Mentality-materiality has the meaning of "simultaneous arising" because mentality and materiality arise simultaneously at the moment of rebirth-linking, and in particular cases during the course of existence.[14] They are "separable" since there is no association of mentality with materiality or of materiality with mentality.[15] That they are "inseparable" should be construed for certain factors of mentality in connection with other factors of mentality and for certain factors of materiality in connection with other factors of materiality. Inseparability intended as simultaneous arising and simultaneous cessation is found between the factors of materiality occurring in a single material cluster. Or else, materiality and mentality are separable because in one-constituent and four-constituent existence, respectively, each occurs completely disconnected from the other, and they are inseparable because in five-constituent existence they occur together.[16] Mentality (*nāma*) has the meaning of "bending" (*namana*) in the sense of being directed to an object. Materiality (*rūpa*) has the meaning of "deformation" (*ruppanā*) in the sense of undergoing alteration through the encounter with adverse conditions.[17]

The sense bases such as the eye, etc. "possess objective domains" since they have the power of illumination, the capacity to reveal the objects such as visible forms, etc. which come into their range. The "soullessness" (*nijjīvaṭṭha*) of feeling is deep because of the strength of the adherence to the idea that a self feels.

The intrinsic nature of these states such as ignorance, etc. is itself "penetration" in the sense that it is penetrated. For it was said in the Introduction (to the commentary to the Dīgha Nikāya): "Penetration is the undistorted intrinsic nature, i.e. the particular characteristic to be penetrated in the different phenomena referred to in various places" (I. p. 20). This intrinsic nature of ignorance, etc. is deep in the sense that it is unfathomable, for it does not allow one without knowledge to find a footing in it. It can only be penetrated by means of undeluded penetration through the knowledge pertaining to the noble path.

CY. All this [the entire depth of dependent arising, which is briefly fourfold but in detail with numerous divisions] appeared clear to the Elder Ānanda [because he was endowed with the four factors mentioned above]. Thus the Exalted One, extolling him, said: "Do not say so, Ānanda!" [494] This is the purport: "Ānanda, you have great wisdom and lucid knowledge. Thus dependent arising, though deep, seems clear to you. Therefore do not say: 'Does it appear clear only to myself or to others as well?'."

Penetration is the undistorted intrinsic nature

4. The Restraining of Ānanda

CY. It was said (p. 61): "The Exalted One says 'Do not say so, Ānanda!' ... to restrain the Venerable Ānanda." This is the purport: "Ānanda, do not say 'to myself it seems as clear as clear can be.' If it seems 'as clear as clear can be' to you, then why didn't you become a stream-enterer on your own instead of penetrating the path of stream-entry only in dependence on the method given by me? Ānanda, if only nibbāna is deep, and the principle of conditionality is clear to you, then why haven't you uprooted four defilements—the two gross fetters of sensual lust and aversion and the two gross underlying tendencies of sensual lust and aversion—and realized the fruit of a once-returner? Why haven't you uprooted those same four defilements in their residual form and realized the fruit of a non-returner? Why haven't you uprooted eight defilements—the five subtle fetters of desire for fine-material and immaterial existence, conceit, restlessness, and ignorance, along with the underlying tendencies of desire for existence, conceit, and ignorance—and realized arahatship?

"Why didn't you fulfil the perfections for one incalculable period and 100,000 aeons and penetrate the knowledge of a chief disciple, like Sāriputta and Moggallāna? Why didn't you fulfil the perfections for two incalculable periods and 100,000 aeons and penetrate the knowledge of a paccekabuddha's enlightenment? If this appears so completely clear to you, then why didn't you fulfil the perfections for four, eight, or sixteen incalculable periods and 100,000 aeons and realize the omniscient knowledge like the Buddhas? Don't you have any use for these distinguished achievements?

"See your mistake! You, a disciple possessing limited knowledge, say of this extremely deep principle of conditionality, 'It appears clear to me.' This statement of yours goes contrary to the explanation of the Buddhas. It is not right for such a bhikkhu to say something going contrary to the explanation of the Buddhas.

"Ānanda, didn't I spend four incalculable periods and 100,000 aeons striving to penetrate this principle of conditionality? There is no gift that I did not give, no perfection that I did not fulfil, to penetrate the principle of conditionality. Resolved upon penetrating the principle of conditionality, [495] I dispersed the army of Māra as though it were powerless, but even then the great earth did not move an inch. It did not move in the first watch of the night when I recollected my past lives or in the middle watch of the night when I attained the divine eye. But in the last watch of the night, at dawn, as soon as I saw: 'Ignorance is a condition for volitional formations through nine modes,' this ten thousandfold world-system, sounding like a brass gong beaten by an iron rod, let loose a hundred roars, a thousand roars, and it shook like a drop of water on a lotus leaf struck by the wind. So deep, Ānanda, is this dependent arising, and so deep its appearance."

SUB. CY. (In the enumeration of the defilements), admittedly sensual lust and aversion themselves are, in denotation, both the fetters of sensual lust and aversion and the underlying tendencies of sensual lust and aversion. But still "fetter" (*saṁyojana*) has one meaning as the state of binding, while "underlying tendency" (*anusaya*) has another meaning, that of gaining strength in the mental continuum because of being unabandoned. Making this distinction in functions the basis for a division, the commentator says "four defilements." The same method applies to the other cases as well.

He shows that the penetration of the truths by the achievement of the higher paths occurs by way of penetrating the principle of conditionality. Then he shows that, in a similar way, the penetration of the truths by the achievement of a disciple's enlightenment, a paccekabuddha's enlightenment, and the perfect enlightenment (of a Buddha) also occurs by way of penetrating the principle of conditionality.

For great bodhisattas who have formed their aspirations, a difference is recognized in the time required to accumulate their collections (of merits and knowledge) for enlightenment. This difference is based on the quality of their energy, whether superior, middling, or inferior. Showing this difference, the commentator says "four, eight, or sixteen incalculable periods."

"Striving to penetrate the principle of conditionality": by this he speaks specifically about the accumulation of the collection of knowledge, the fulfilment of the perfection of wisdom. All merit is a decisive support for this. Therefore, for all the great bodhisattas, their collection of merit is only for the sake of their collection of knowledge, since (it is knowledge) which has the capacity to bring the full achievement of the perfect enlightenment. Thus he says; "There is no gift," etc.

Now to show the supreme depth of dependent arising indirectly, by showing the great spiritual power involved in the penetration of the principle of conditionality, it is said: "As soon as I saw: 'Ignorance is a condition for volitional formations through nine modes.'" Ignorance is a condition for volitional formations through the nine modes: arising, occurrence, sign, accumulation, conjunction, impediment, origin, cause, and condition.[18] So too are the volitional formations for consciousness, etc. For it is said in the *Paṭisambhidāmagga*: "How is wisdom in the discernment of conditions the knowledge of the structure of phenomena? Ignorance is the structuring factor for volitional formations as their arising, occurrence, sign, accumulation, conjunct, impediment, origin, cause, and condition. Through these nine modes ignorance is the condition and the volitional formations are conditionally arisen," etc. (Pṭs.i,50).

Therein, "nine modes" are nine modes of exercising the conditioning nature. "Arising": that from which the effect arises, the cause for the arising of the effect. Volitional formations arise when there is ignorance, not when ignorance is absent; thus ignorance is a condition for volitional formations as their arising. Similarly, volitional formations occur and are guided when there is ignorance, (thus ignorance is the cause for their occurrence and their sign). Ignorance is the condition for the way they throw beings into the realms of existence and for the way they accumulate for the arising of their effect, (thus ignorance is an accumulation). It is a condition for the way they connect and join together with their own effect, (thus it is a conjunct), and for the way they impede the mental continuum in which they have arisen, (thus it is an impediment). They originate, arise, in the encounter with other conditions, (thus ignorance is their origin). It sends forth volitional formations and becomes the reason for them, (thus ignorance is their cause). The volitional formations come forth and occur in dependence upon ignorance, (thus ignorance is their condition). Thus these nine modes should be understood as the distinct ways ignorance exercises a causative nature in relation to the volitional formations. The same method should be applied to the volitional formations, etc. as the arising, etc. for consciousness, etc. The "structuring factor" (*ṭhiti*) is the cause.

This passage shows the Buddha's undertaking of the discernment of conditions at the time (of his enlightenment). And that undertaking followed the established pattern. It occurred to himself in the same way it occurred to the great bodhisattas of the past as they sat at the foot of the Bodhi tree.

BECAUSE OF NOT UNDERSTANDING AND NOT PENETRATING THIS DHAMMA ...

CY. "This Dhamma" is the Dhamma of conditions. "Because of not understanding" (*ananubodhā*): because of not understanding it by way of the full understanding of the known. "(Because of) not penetrating" (*appaṭivedhā*): because of not penetrating it by way of the full understanding by scrutinization and the full understanding by abandoning.[19]

Full understanding:
.by scrutinization & foundation" thanks of Conditions
.by abandoning perception of permanence

suppresses opposing states **

The Commentarial Exegesis   71

SUB. CY. "This Dhamma" is dependent arising. Since this is, in denotation, the set of causes for the phenomena springing from causes, he calls it "the Dhamma of conditions." The meaning is: the conditionality of (the conditioning phenomena) such as birth, etc. with respect to (the conditioned phenomena) such as aging and death, etc.

The delimitation of mentality-materiality and the discernment of conditions do not come about by the mere first interpretation of phenomena, but by the recurrent arising of knowledge about them called "repeated understanding." Showing the absence of both (these kinds of knowledge), the commentator says "not understanding it by way of the full understanding of the known."

The full understanding by scrutinization and the full understanding by abandoning are included within insight and the noble path. Insight includes them because it occurs as the abandoning of the perception of permanence, etc. and it is itself the penetrating of phenomena. And the full understanding by scrutinization is its foundation, for it suppresses the opposing states, thereby enabling insight to acquire precision and lucidity. The noble path includes them because it occurs by way of comprehension through full understanding and abandoning.[20] Showing the absence of both kinds of penetration, the commentator says "not penetrating it by way of the full understanding by scrutinization and the full understanding by abandoning."

BECOME LIKE A TANGLED SKEIN (*tantākulajātā*)

tangled rope.

CY. When weaver's yarn which has been badly kept and gnawed by mice becomes tangled all over, it is difficult to distinguish its beginning and end and to straighten it out from beginning to end. Similarly, beings have stumbled over the principle of conditionality; they have become tangled and bewildered and are unable to straighten it out. However, it is possible for a person to straighten out a tangled skein by relying on his own personal ability. But except for the two kinds of bodhisattas [those who will become paccekabuddhas and perfect Buddhas], other beings are incapable of straightening out the principle of conditionality on their own [without the instructions of another]. And as a tangled skein, moistened with grease and worked over with a comb, becomes clustered and knotted all over, in the same way these beings who have stumbled over conditions and cannot set them straight become confused and bound up in knots over the sixty-two views. For all those who rely on views are unable to straighten out the principle of conditionality.

** thereby enabling insight to acquire precision & lucidity

*Why it is difficult to see a beginning or an end

SUB. CY. "Stumbled over the principle of conditionality": having missed the middle path, they have fallen into the two extremes (of eternalism and annihilationism). "Stumbled over conditions": stumbled by assuming the conditioning phenomena to be permanent, happiness, and self, when in their intrinsic nature they are impermanent, suffering, and non-self. "Unable to straighten out the principle of conditionality": because they do not give up their assumptions of permanence, etc., they are unable to straighten out their own views regarding conditions, and therefore they become tied in knots by way of the bodily knot of dogmatic adherences.[21]

LIKE A KNOTTED BALL OF THREAD (*kulāganṭhikajātā*)

CY. A "knotted ball of thread" is greased weavers' thread. Some say that the term signifies a bird's nest. Both of these are tangled and difficult to straighten out from beginning to end. The meaning may be interpreted by the method of the previous simile. [496]

LIKE MATTED RUSHES AND REEDS

beaten down grasses

CY. These grasses are beaten and made into a rope. If one takes that rope when it has become old and has fallen somewhere, it is difficult to distinguish the beginning and end of those grasses and to straighten them out from beginning to end. However, it is possible for a person to straighten them out by relying on his own personal ability. But except for the two kinds of bodhisattas, other beings are incapable of straightening out the principle of conditionality on their own. Thus this generation, being unable to straighten out the principle of conditionality, has become like a ball of thread and does not pass beyond saṁsāra with its plane of misery, unfortunate destinations, and lower realms.

The plane of misery includes the hells, the animal realm, the realm of afflicted spirits, and the host of titans. All these are called the "plane of misery" because of the absence of the joy consisting in progress, the "unfortunate destinations" because they have gone to suffering, and the "lower realms" because they have fallen from the heights of happiness. Regarding saṁsāra, it is said:

The succession of aggregates,
Elements and sense bases
Continuing uninterrupted—
That is called saṁsāra.

This generation does not pass beyond all that, does not overcome it. But rather, (unable to straighten out the principle of conditionality), it goes from death to rebirth and from rebirth to death. Passing away and taking rebirth-linking over and over, like a ship on the ocean driven by a storm or like an ox yoked to a mill-wheel, it only revolves in the three realms of existence, the four modes of origin, the five destinations, the seven stations of consciousness, and the nine abodes of beings.

The Exalted One, it should be understood, said all this to restrain the Venerable Ānanda.

5. Dependent Arising

2. **CY.** Now this sutta is bound together by two phrases: (1) "This dependent arising, Ānanda, is deep," and (2) "This generation has become like a tangled skein." Therefore, in order to show the depth of the principle of conditionality first, as the sequel to the phrase "This dependent arising, Ānanda, is deep," the Buddha begins the teaching by saying:

ĀNANDA, IF ONE IS ASKED: "ARE AGING AND DEATH DUE TO A SPECIFIC CONDITION?" (*atthi idappaccayā jarāmaraṇaṁ*)

CY. This is the meaning: "Ānanda, if a wise person is asked: 'Are aging and death due to a specific condition? That is, is there a condition for aging and death through which aging and death come to be?' [497] he should not remain silent or say, 'This has not been explained by the Tathāgata,' as he would if were asked a question to be set aside, such as 'Are the soul and the body the same?' He should say unequivocally: 'They are,' just as, if he were asked whether the eye is eternal or non-eternal, he would say unequivocally: 'It is non-eternal.' If he is further asked: 'Through what condition is there aging and death? What is that condition through which aging and death come to be?' he should say: 'With birth as condition there is aging and death.'" The same method applies to all the remaining cases (in the passage being explained).

WITH MENTALITY-MATERIALITY AS CONDITION THERE IS CONTACT.

CY. When it is said (in the usual formulation of dependent arising), "With the six sense bases as condition there is contact," inclusion is made of only the six kinds of resultant contact, that is, eye-contact, etc.

But here the Buddha wishes to show the distinct conditionally arisen (kinds of contact) whether or not they are included by the phrase "With the six sense bases as condition there is contact"; and he also wishes to show a distinctive condition for contact different from the six sense bases. Therefore he says: "With mentality-materiality as condition there is contact."

What has the Exalted One explained in this section of the sutta? He has explained the source (cause) of the conditions.[22] For this sutta is called "The Great Discourse on Causation" because it is explained to disentagle and unravel conditions.

SUB. CY. "Inclusion is made of only the six kinds of resultant contact": because in numerous suttas and in the Abhidhamma (the factors of dependent arising) that begin with consciousness and end in feeling are treated as resultants, and thus contact is usually interpreted as including only the resultant kinds of contact. "Whether or not they are included by the phrase": those included are the six kinds of resultant contact; those not included are the non-resultant kinds of contact, i.e. wholesome, unwholesome, and functional contacts.

When the six sense bases are mentioned, only the internal sense bases are included; thus the Buddha "wishes to show a distinctive condition for contact different from the six sense bases." For the six sense bases, such as the eye, etc., are not the only condition for contact. Material phenomena such as the visible form base and mental phenomena such as eye-consciousness are also conditions. As it is said: "In dependence upon the eye and visible forms there arises eye-consciousness. The meeting of the three is contact."

"He has explained the source (cause) of the conditions": the conditions are the conditioning phenomena such as birth, etc. He has explained their causality (*nidānatta*) in relation to (the conditioned phenomena) such as aging and death, etc., that is, he has explained their unequivocal conditioning nature. To show that there is no deviation in their conditioning nature, the teaching in the subsequent sections that begin "It was said" (§§ 4ff.) is presented. By the two terms "disentangle" and "unravel" the commentator shows the absence of entanglement. Therefore, since the great subject of conditional-causation (*paccayanidāna*) is explained here free from entanglement and confusion, this sutta is entitled "The Great Discourse on Causation," owing to the absence of variability.

4. **CY.** Now to show the real, undelusive, invariable conditioning nature of the various conditions, the Exalted One says:

IT WAS SAID: "WITH BIRTH AS CONDITION THERE IS AGING AND DEATH," ETC.

SUB. CY. The conditioning nature is "real" (*tatha*), true, because each particular effect originates through its appropriate conditions, neither more nor less. Or else that principle is "real" because once their conditions reach completeness, there is no non-origination of the phenomena due to be produced through them even for a moment. It is "undelusive" (*avitatha*), undeceptive, devoid of deceptiveness, since no phenomenon arises through the conditions appropriate to some other phenomenon. It is "invariable" (*anaññatha*) because of the absence of variability.[23]

CY. [498] "Gods" (*devā*): gods by rebirth. "Celestials" (*gandhabbā*): deities dwelling in roots, tree-trunks, etc. "Spirits" (*yakkhā*): non-human beings. "Demons" (*bhūtā*): whatever beings are generated.

SUB. CY. "Gods by rebirth": from the heaven of the four great kings up to the highest plane of existence. "Celestials": the retinue of the great king Dhataraṭṭha. "Spirits": the retinue of the great king Vessavaṇa. "Demons": the retinue of the great king Virūḷhaka.[24]

THE CAUSE, SOURCE, ORIGIN, AND CONDITION ...

CY. All these words are synonyms for the reason (*kāraṇa*). For the reason is called "cause" (*hetu*) because it comes forth in order to produce its effect; the "source" (*nidāna*), because it brings forth its effect as if commanding "come and take it"; the "origin" (*samudaya*), because the effect originates from it; and the "condition" (*paccaya*), because the effect occurs in dependence upon it. Birth is a condition for aging and death under the heading of decisive support (*upanissaya*).[25]

SUB. CY. Birth is a decisive support for aging and death because the latter occurs when it has occurred and does not occur when it has not occurred.

5. WITH EXISTENCE AS CONDITION THERE IS BIRTH.

CY. Therein, sense-sphere existence includes everything between the Avīci hell as the lower limit and the "gods who control the creations of others" as the upper limit.[26] That is the method of interpretation in regard to rebirth-existence. But here existence should be interpreted as kamma-existence, for this is a condition for birth under the heading of decisive support.[27]

SUB. CY. *Query*: Isn't it true that rebirth-existence is also a decisive support condition for birth?

Reply: That is true, but it is not primary. Kamma-existence, on the other hand, is the primary condition (for birth) since it has the nature of generating birth. Sense-sphere existence, as the condition for birth, is the kamma leading to (rebirth into) sense-sphere existence. The same method applies to fine-material and immaterial existence.

6. WITH CLINGING AS CONDITION THERE IS EXISTENCE.

CY. Here clinging to sense pleasures is a condition for the three kinds of kamma-existence and also for the three kinds of rebirth-existence; so too the remaining kinds of clinging. Thus twenty-four kinds of existence have clinging as condition.[28] But literally the twelve kinds of kamma-existence obtain here. The clingings are a condition for these under the heading of decisive support as well as under the heading of conascence (*sahajāta*).

SUB. CY. "Three kinds of kamma-existence": sense-sphere, (fine-material, and immaterial) kamma-existence. "Three kinds of rebirth-existence": sense-sphere, (fine-material, and immaterial) rebirth-existence.

"But literally the twelve kinds of kamma-existence obtain here": since clinging is a condition for rebirth-existence through its nature as a condition for kamma-existence, not otherwise, it is directly a condition for kamma-existence.

"Under the heading of conascence": clinging is a condition for the unwholesome kamma conascent with itself under the heading of conascence; it is a condition for other (unwholesome kamma) under the heading of decisive support, by way of being a proximate decisive support condition, etc. But it is a condition for wholesome kamma only under the heading of decisive support. And here "under the heading of conascence" is said to show that such conditions as mutuality, support, association, presence, and non-disappearance, etc. are included by the conascence condition. So too "under the heading of decisive support" is said to include collectively object decisive support, proximate decisive support, and natural decisive support.

7. WITH CRAVING AS CONDITION THERE IS CLINGING.

CY. Craving is a condition for clinging under the heading of conascence as well as under the heading of decisive support. [499]

SUB. CY. Here craving is a condition for clinging to sense pleasures only under the heading of decisive support, but it is a condition for the remaining kinds of clinging under the headings of both conascence and decisive support. The factors that begin with consciousness and end in feeling are to be treated as resultants.

8. THIS IS ... THE CONDITION FOR CRAVING, NAMELY, FEELING.

CY. Here resultant feeling is a condition for craving under the heading of decisive support, the other (i.e. non-resultant feeling) in the other way, too (i.e. under the heading of conascence).

9. **CY.** To this extent the Exalted One has shown the previous craving (*purimataṇhā*) that becomes the root of the round. Now, as if striking someone on the back or grabbing him by the hair and pulling him away while he wails, the Exalted One pulls the teaching down from its usual sequence and speaks the present passage to show, by way of nine terms, obsessional craving (*samudācārataṇhā*).

SUB. CY. "Previous craving": the craving completed in the previous existence. "Pulls the teaching down from its usual sequence": in the sequence for teaching dependent arising by the method that has come down in other suttas, contact is cited as the condition for feeling. Thus, immediately after saying "This is the condition for craving, namely, feeling," the Exalted One would say: "It was said: 'With contact as condition there is feeling.'" But here he does not enter upon that sequence; rather, by showing obsessional craving, he teaches the phenomena rooted in craving, pulling the teaching down from its usual sequence as if to teach, forcefully and emphatically, that there is no occurrence (of craving) for one who sees that teaching.

THUS, ĀNANDA, IN DEPENDENCE UPON FEELING THERE IS CRAVING ...

CY. Within that (obsessional) craving there are two kinds of craving: acquisitive craving (*esanataṇhā*) and possessive craving (*esitataṇhā*). Acquisitive craving is the craving because of which one travels along rough and rugged paths seeking wealth. Possessive craving is the craving for those things which have been sought after and obtained. Both of these are designations for obsessional craving. Therefore, this twofold craving arises in dependence upon feeling.

SUB. CY. Acquisitive craving is the craving which motivates the pursuit of wealth, possessive craving the craving which arises for the wealth that has been pursued. Obsessional craving is craving that occurs by way of manifestation.[29] "This twofold craving arises in dependence upon feeling": pursuit in order to acquire wealth not yet obtained and achieving ownership of that which has been gained.

CY. "Pursuit" is the pursuit of objects such as visible forms, etc. "Gain" is the obtaining of such objects, for that occurs when there is pursuit. "Decision-making" is fourfold, by way of knowledge, craving, views, and thought.[30] Therein, decision-making as knowledge is referred to in the passage: "One should know how to decide on happiness. Knowing how to decide on happiness, one should be devoted to inner happiness" (M.139; iii,233). Decision-making as craving is the "hundred and eight reflections due to craving" (A.iv,199). Decision-making as views is the sixty-two views. Since it is said "Desire, lord of gods, has its source in thought" (D.21; ii,277), in this sutta here "decision-making" is intended as thought. For having gained something, one thinks of it as desirable or undesirable, beautiful or ugly, and then decides: "This much will be for visible forms, this much for sounds, etc. This is for me, this for others. This I will use, this I will keep." Thus it is said: "In dependence upon gain there is decision-making."

"Desire and lust": because of unwholesome thoughts, weak and strong lust arises towards the object thought about. This here is craving. Desire is a weak form of lust.

"Attachment" is strong conviction (with the ideas) of "I" and "mine." "Possessiveness" is taking possession by way of craving and views. "Stinginess" is unwillingness to share with others. [500] "Safeguarding" is guarding well by locking one's door, keeping things in a safe, etc. The "taking up of clubs" is taking up a club to restrain others, the "taking up of weapons" is taking up a sword, etc. "Conflicts" may be bodily or verbal; "quarrels" come first and "disputes" afterwards. "Insulting speech" is disrespectful speech.

10-18. **CY.** Now to show obsessional craving in reverse order, in these sections the Buddha traces the teaching back. Therein (in §18), "craving for sense pleasures" is craving for visible forms, etc., which arises as lust for the five strands of sense pleasure. "Craving for existence" is desire accompanied by the eternalist view, "craving for non-existence" desire accompanied by the annihilationist view.

THESE TWO PHENOMENA, BEING A DUALITY, CONVERGE INTO A UNITY IN FEELING.

CY. "These two phenomena": craving which is a root of the round and obsessional craving. "Being a duality": though unified by their characteristic of craving, they form two sections insofar as craving is both a root of the round and an obsession, and through these they converge into a unity in feeling. The meaning is: they have a single condition in that they both occur with feeling as condition.

"Convergence" is threefold: convergence by descent, convergence by conascence, and convergence by condition.[31] Convergence by descent is referred to in the passage: "All these converge upon sense pleasures" (untraced); convergence by conascence in the passage: "These phenomena, friend, are rooted in desire, originate from contact, and converge upon feeling" (A.VIII,83; iv,339); convergence by condition in the present passage: "being a duality, (they) converge into a unity in feeling."

19. WITH CONTACT AS CONDITION THERE IS FEELING.

CY. Eye-contact, etc. are all resultant contacts only. Excepting the four supramundane resultant contacts, the remainder number thirty-two.[32] Herein, contact is a condition for feeling in many ways.

SUB. CY. "Resultant contacts only": interpreting the factors that begin with consciousness and end in feeling as resultants, all contact is divided by way of the door of its arising. The supramundane contacts are excluded because this is an explanation of the round.

"Contact is a condition for feeling in many ways": in the five sense doors, the fivefold sense contact, such as eye-contact, etc., is a condition in eight ways—as conascence, mutuality, support, kamma-resultant, nutriment, association, presence, and non-disappearance conditions—for the five kinds of feeling that take the sensitive matter of the eye, etc. as their basis.[33] The fivefold sense contact, such as eye-contact, etc., is a condition in only one way—as decisive support condition—for the remaining sense-sphere resultant feelings occurring in each sense door by way of the reception, investigation, and registration (states of consciousness).[34]

In the mind door, its conascent mind-contact is a condition in the aforementioned eight ways for the sense-sphere resultant feelings occurring by way of the registration consciousness; the same for the resultant feelings of the three planes occurring by way of the rebirth-linking, life-continuum, and death states of consciousness. But the mind-contact associated with the mind-door adverting consciousness is a condition in only one way—as decisive support condition—for the sense-sphere feelings occurring in the mind-door by way of the registration consciousness.

* Mentally bending in the direction of an object

20. THOSE QUALITIES, TRAITS, SIGNS, AND INDICATORS THROUGH WHICH THERE IS A DESCRIPTION OF THE MENTAL BODY …

CY. The mutually dissimilar intrinsic natures [of feeling, perception, mental formations, and consciousness] are called "qualities" (*ākāra*). They are also called "traits" (*liṅga*) because, when carefully looked at, they betray the concealed meanings (of their base); "signs" (*nimitta*), because they are causes for perceiving particular things; and "indicators" (*uddesa*), because they are to be indicated in particular ways. [501]

SUB. CY. "The mutually dissimilar intrinsic natures": the natures of experiencing, perceiving, volitionally forming, and cognizing.[35] These are called "qualities" because they qualify (their base) and are discerned as the mutually distinct features of being what is felt, etc. (in the case of feeling).

"They betray the concealed meanings": they make known the particular concealed, unapparent meanings, such as the meaning of being immaterial, the meaning of bending in the direction of an object, etc. (in the case of the mental body).

"They are causes for perceiving particular things": they are causes for taking notice of their meaning of being immaterial, etc. "Signs": through these (the meaning) is signalled and inferred.

"They are to be indicated in particular ways": they are to be explained through the mode of being immaterial and through the mode of being what is felt, etc.

IF THOSE QUALITIES, ETC. … WERE ALL ABSENT, WOULD DESIGNATION-CONTACT BE DISCERNED IN THE MATERIAL BODY?

CY. This is the meaning here: "Ānanda, when there are present those qualities, traits, signs, and indicators through which there is a description of the 'mental body,' the mental group; that is, when there is present feeling's quality, trait, and sign of being what is felt, and its indicator 'feeling'; when there is present perception's quality, trait, and sign of perceiving, and its indicator 'perception'; when there is present the mental formations' quality, trait, and sign of volition, and their indicator 'volition'; when there is present consciousness's quality, trait, and sign of cognizing, and its indicator 'consciousness'—then there is a description of the mental body thus: 'This is the mental body.' But when the

"nama" mental in the sense of bending
"namana" in the direction of an object

causes for the description of the mental body—the quality, etc. of feeling, etc.—are all absent, would designation-contact be discerned in the material body? Designation-contact (*adhivacanasamphassa*) is synonymous with mind-contact (*manosamphassa*), which arises in the mind-door taking as its basis the four mental aggregates. Would that be discerned in the material body? Would it arise taking as its basis one or another of the five kinds of sensitive matter?"

The Venerable Ānanda replies: "Certainly not, venerable sir," rejecting the arising of (mind-contact) from the material body (alone), just as one would the arising of a mango fruit from a rose-apple tree when mango trees are absent.

SUB. CY. The "mental group" is the assemblage of immaterial phenomena comprised in the four mental aggregates—feeling, perception, mental formations, and consciousness. It is designated "mental" (*nāma*) in the sense of bending (*namana*) in the direction of an object.

"There is a description of the mental body": there is a describing of it as "mental body," "immaterial cluster," "immaterial aggregates," etc. Volition is stated to be the quality of mental formations because it is primary among the phenomena included in the aggregate of mental formations.

"Taking as its basis the four mental aggregates": taking as its basis the phenomena serving as the support condition (for that contact)—feeling, perception, consciousness, volition, etc., which are referred to (by way of their grouping into) the four mental aggregates. Though this method also applies to the five physical sense doors, "in the mind-door" is specified.

"Designation-contact is synonymous with mind-contact": the latter gains the name "designation-contact" because it is apprehended by means of (its functions of) designation and description. It is "discerned in the material body" because, in five-constituent existence, it is found occurring with the support of the heart-basis.[36]

"Would it arise taking as its basis one or another of the five kinds of sensitive matter?": this is not recognized here, as is illustrated by showing the impossibility (of designation-contact in the material body) when feeling and the other mental factors are rejected. For without the support of feeling, etc., it is impossible for mind-contact to occur taking as its basis the five kinds of sensitive matter. By means of the example of the mango fruit he shows the inevitable conclusion: "When the necessary cause for the arising of an effect is absent, the effect never arises from some other cause not appropriate to its arising."

IF THOSE QUALITIES, ETC. THROUGH WHICH THERE IS A DESCRIPTION OF THE MATERIAL BODY WERE ALL ABSENT, WOULD IMPINGEMENT-CONTACT BE DISCERNED IN THE MENTAL BODY?

CY. In this second question, the terms "qualities," etc., should be understood to mean the quality, trait, and sign of deformation,[37] and the indicator "material form." Impingement-contact is the contact which arises taking as its basis the impingent aggregate of material form.[38] Here the Elder Ānanda replies: "Certainly not, venerable sir," rejecting the arising of (impingement-contact) from the mental body (alone), just as one would the arising of a rose-apple fruit from a mango tree when rose-apple trees are absent.

SUB. CY. The quality of deformation is manifest deterioration in the encounter with adverse conditions. Or it is the cause for the deterioration of what exists in one's own continuum in the event (of such encounters). The quality of deformation is itself also a "trait" because it betrays the concealed meanings such as basis, impingement, etc.; it is a "sign" because it is a cause for perceiving particular things; and an "indicator" because it is to be indicated in particular ways. "Impingement" is the impinging, one upon the other, of object and basis. The contact produced from that impingement is called "impingement-contact" (*paṭighasamphassa*).

IF THOSE QUALITIES, ETC. THROUGH WHICH THERE IS A DESCRIPTION OF THE MENTAL BODY AND THE MATERIAL BODY WERE ALL ABSENT, WOULD EITHER DESIGNATION-CONTACT OR IMPINGEMENT-CONTACT BE DISCERNED?

CY. This third question is stated in terms of both. The Elder replies: "Certainly not, venerable sir," rejecting the arising of either of the two kinds of contact in the absence of mentality-materiality, just as one would the arising of mangoes and rose-apples in space.

SUB. CY. "In terms of both": in terms of both supports, the mental body and the material body, and in terms of both kinds of contact, designation-contact and impingement-contact.

IF THOSE QUALITIES, ETC. THROUGH WHICH THERE IS A DESCRIPTION OF MENTALITY-MATERIALITY WERE ALL ABSENT, WOULD CONTACT BE DISCERNED?

CY. Having shown the conditions for the two kinds of contact separately, now the Exalted One poses the fourth question in order to show, without making distinctions, that mentality-materiality is the condition for the two [kinds of contact].

THIS IS THE CAUSE ... AND CONDITION FOR CONTACT, NAMELY, MENTALITY-MATERIALITY.

CY. The meaning is: "The mentality-materiality occurring in the six doors, this is the cause, this is the condition, [for the two kinds of contact]." For in the eye-door, the eye and visible form objects are materiality and the aggregates associated [with contact] are mentality; the same holds, with appropriate changes, in regard to the other physical sense doors. Thus this fivefold contact [by way of eye-contact, etc.] is still "contact with mentality-materiality as condition." [502] In the mind-door, too, the heart-basis and any material object are materiality, the phenomena associated [with contact] and any immaterial object are mentality. Thus mind-contact, too, is "contact with mentality-materiality as condition." Mentality-materiality is a condition for this [contact] in many ways.

SUB. CY. The aggregates associated with contact are those of feeling, etc. Adverting should also be included by the mentioning of the associated aggregates, since that is inseparable.

"Mentality-materiality is a condition for this contact in many ways": thus resultant mentality is a condition for the numerous kinds of resultant mind-contact in seven ways—as conascence, mutuality, support, kamma-resultant, association, presence, and non-disappearance conditions. Whatever functions here (in the resultant mentality) as nutriment is a nutriment condition; whatever functions as a faculty is a faculty condition. Non-resultant mentality is a condition for non-resultant mind-contact in all the above ways except for kamma-resultant condition.

Materiality, classified (by way of the internal sense bases) into the eye-base, etc., is a condition for the (corresponding) fivefold contact, eye-contact, etc., in six ways—as support, prenascence, faculty, dissociation, presence, and non-disappearance conditions. Classified (by way of the external sense bases) into the visible form-base, etc., materiality is a condition for the same fivefold contact in four ways—as object, prenascence, presence, and non-disappearance conditions.

(The five external sense bases classified into) the visible form-base, etc. and mental objects are a condition in only one way—as object condition—for mind-contact.[39] The materiality of the heart-basis is a condition for mind-contact in five ways—as support, prenascence, dissociation, presence, and non-disappearance conditions.

Thus mentality-materiality is a condition for this contact in many ways.

21. IF CONSCIOUSNESS WERE NOT TO DESCEND INTO THE MOTHER'S WOMB ...

CY. If, after having entered, it were not to occur by way of rebirth-linking.

SUB. CY. It is said in the text "were not to descend into the mother's womb" in order to show separately that consciousness, at its first arising, is the distinctive condition for mentality-materiality. Though the rebirth-linking of the embryo is spoken of as if it descends into the mother's womb from outside, the phrase actually denotes the first arising of the aggregates there in accordance with conditions.

WOULD MENTALITY-MATERIALITY TAKE SHAPE IN THE WOMB?

CY. If there were no rebirth-linking consciousness, would the remaining bare mentality-materiality occur in the mother's womb, "taking shape" by developing through the various embryonic stages?

SUB. CY. "The remaining bare mentality-materiality": the remaining mentality-materiality only, without consciousness.

IF, AFTER DESCENDING INTO THE WOMB, CONSCIOUSNESS WERE TO DEPART ...

CY. If, after descending by way of rebirth-linking, it were to perish by way of death; that is, if it were to cease. This cessation does not come about through the ceasing of the rebirth-linking consciousness itself, nor through the subsequent ceasing of the second and third (states of consciousness). For thirty kamma-born material phenomena are produced originating along with the rebirth-linking consciousness. While they endure, sixteen moments of life-continuum consciousness arise and cease.[40] During this time [during these sixteen moments of consciousness] there is no obstacle to the child who has taken rebirth-linking or to the mother. This is called "the period of safety." If the material phenomena originating along with the rebirth-linking consciousness can provide a condition for the seventeenth life-continuum consciousness, the course of existence occurs and the current (of material phenomena) continues. But if they cannot provide a condition, the course of existence does not occur and the current does not continue. This is called "departing" and it was in reference to this that the Buddha said: "If, after descending, consciousness were to depart."

SUB. CY. "If consciousness were to depart": if it were to undergo destruction, the cutting off of the continuity, i.e. death.

"There is no obstacle": in the case of the child there is certainly no obstacle, no danger of death, since it is impossible for the death-consciousness to occur then,[41] but how is there no danger of death for the mother? Because until that time has lapsed, it is impossible for the act of conception to bring about death. Thus it is called "the period of safety," i.e. from death.

"The material phenomena originating along with the rebirth-linking consciousness": he speaks of the kamma-born material phenomena arisen at the moment of conception, for those are literally called "the material phenomena originating along with the rebirth-linking consciousness." But not those originated by temperature, since those originate subsequent to the arising of the rebirth-linking consciousness. Material phenomena born of consciousness and those born of nutriment do not originate then at all.

The material phenomena originating along with the rebirth-linking consciousness are threefold: those originating at its arising moment, those originating at its duration moment, and those originating at its dissolution moment.[42] Those originating at its arising moment cease at the arising moment of the seventeenth life-continuum consciousness; those originating at its duration moment cease at the duration moment (of the seventeenth life-continuum consciousness); and those originating at its dissolution moment cease at the dissolution moment (of the seventeenth life-continuum consciousness). One phenomenon undergoing dissolution cannot be said to become a condition for another phenomenon undergoing dissolution; but it is not impossible in the phases of arising and duration. Thus what is meant by the statement under discussion is this: "If, at the arising and duration moments of the seventeenth life-continuum consciousness, (the material phenomena originating along with the rebirth-linking consciousness) can provide a condition for it by means of (those material phenomena) still standing...."[43] For in five-constituent existence the mental body occurs sustained by the material body.

"The course of existence occurs" (*pavatti pavattati*): this is said referring to the strengthening of consciousness by the material phenomena. "And the current continues" (*paveṇī ghaṭīyati*): the current of kamma-born material phenomena originating at forty-eight moments continues on in succession. For first the rebirth-linking consciousness occurs; then (the process continues) up to the sixteenth life-continuum consciousness. Each of these has three sub-moments: arising, duration, and dissolution. At each of the three sub-moments of each consciousness thirty kamma-born material phenomena arise. Thus the sixteen sets of three amount to forty-eight (sub-moments when material phenomena originate). The same method applies to the following moments.

"But if they cannot provide a condition": that is, if the material phenomena originating along with the rebirth-linking consciousness cannot provide a condition for the seventeenth life-continuum consciousness. For if the seventeenth consciousness following the rebirth-linking consciousness were to be a death consciousness, kamma-born material phenomena would not arise even at the duration and dissolution moments of the rebirth-linking consciousness, not to speak of the moments of the life-continuum consciousness. In such a case consciousness would not gain a condition, and thus the course of existence would not occur and the current would not continue. It would necessarily be cut off. Thus he says: "This is called 'departing.' "

WOULD MENTALITY-MATERIALITY BE GENERATED INTO THIS PRESENT STATE OF BEING?

CY. "This present state of being" (*itthatta*): the state of the complete five aggregates.

IF THE CONSCIOUSNESS OF A YOUNG BOY OR GIRL WERE TO BE CUT OFF, WOULD MENTALITY-MATERIALITY GROW UP, DEVELOP, AND REACH MATURITY?

CY. The meaning is: "If consciousness were to be cut off, would bare mentality-materiality survive and grow up in the first period of life, develop through the middle period, and reach maturity in the last period? Would it grow up, develop, and reach maturity through ten, twenty, a hundred, or a thousand years?"

THEREFORE, ĀNANDA, THIS IS THE CAUSE ... AND CONDITION FOR MENTALITY-MATERIALITY, NAMELY, CONSCIOUSNESS.

CY. [503] Since consciousness itself is the condition when rebirth-linking takes place in the mother's womb, during the stay in the womb, at the time of leaving the womb, and for ten years and more during the course of existence, "therefore this is the cause, this is the condition for mentality-materiality, namely, consciousness." For consciousness is a condition for mentality-materiality in the way a king, restraining his retinue, might say: "Who was it that made you viceroy and you general? Didn't I do so? For if you could become a viceroy or general by yourself, without my making you such, then we would know your power." In the same way, as it were, consciousness might say to mentality-materiality: "Who is it that made you mentality, you materiality, you mentality-materiality? Didn't I do so? For if you could become mentality, materiality, or mentality-materiality without myself having become a forerunner and taken rebirth-linking in the mother's womb, then we would know your power." Consciousness is a condition for mentality-materiality in many ways.

SUB. CY. The phrase "consciousness itself" is a limiting expression, a term repudiating the self posited by outside (non-Buddhist) thinkers as well as a creator God, etc. But it does not repudiate ignorance, etc. and contact, etc. (the other phenomena conditioning mentality-materiality), since the emphasis of the term is on the exclusion of its intended opposite only.

"Consciousness is a condition for mentality-materiality in many ways." How? Rebirth-linking or any other resultant consciousness is a condition in nine ways—as conascence, mutuality, support, kamma-result, nutriment, faculty, association, presence, and non-disappearance conditions—for resultant mentality, whether at rebirth-linking or in the course of existence, whether it be mixed with materiality or unmixed.

At rebirth-linking it is a condition for the materiality of the heart-basis in nine ways—as conascence, mutuality, support, kamma-result, nutriment, faculty, dissociation, presence, and non-disappearance conditions. It is a condition for the remaining materiality apart from the heart-basis in eight ways—in all the above ways except the mutuality condition. Volitionally formative consciousness is a condition in only one way—as decisive support condition—for the materiality of the non-percipient beings or for kamma-born materiality in five-constituent existence, according to the Suttanta method.

All the remaining types of consciousness, from the first life-continuum consciousness onwards, should be understood to be a condition for mentality-materiality as appropriate. This is a synopsis. The method of assigning the conditions in detail has not been shown since to do so the entire explanation of the "Great Treatise" (i.e. the *Paṭṭhāna*) would have to be brought in.

Query: How is it to be ascertained that at rebirth mentality-materiality occurs with consciousness as condition?

Reply: Both through the suttas and through reasoning (*yutti*). For in the texts, consciousness has come down in many ways as the condition for feeling, etc. As it is said: "Phenomena occur accompanied by consciousness" (Dhs. p. 5). Through reasoning it is understood by inference from consciousness-born materiality seen here that consciousness is also a condition for unseen materiality. For when the mind is calm or disturbed, material phenomena are seen arising in accordance with it (i.e. with the state of mind); and through that which is seen inference is made to the unseen. Accordingly, it can be ascertained through the consciousness-born materiality that is seen here, that consciousness is also a condition for the unseen materiality at rebirth-linking. For in the *Paṭṭhāna* consciousness has come down as the condition for materiality originating from kamma just as it has for materiality originating from consciousness.

22. THEREFORE, ĀNANDA, THIS IS THE CAUSE ... AND CONDITION FOR CONSCIOUSNESS, NAMELY, MENTALITY-MATERIALITY.

CY. (Mentality-materiality is a condition for consciousness) in the way a king's officers, restraining the king, might say: "Who was it that made you king? Didn't we do so? If you could become king alone, without one of us occupying the position of viceroy, another the position of general, then we would see what kind of king you are." In the same way, as it were, mentality-materiality might say to consciousness: "Who is it that made you the rebirth-linking consciousness? Didn't we do so? If you could become a rebirth-linking consciousness without the support of the other three mental aggregates and the heart-basis, then we would see what kind of rebirth-linking consciousness you are." Mentality-materiality is a condition for consciousness in many ways.

SUB. CY. How? At rebirth-linking, mentality is a condition for consciousness in seven ways—as conascence, mutuality, support, kamma-resultant, association, presence, and non-disappearance conditions. Mentality is here a condition in other ways, some as a root-cause condition, some as a nutriment condition.

Non-resultant mentality is a condition in six ways— in all the above ways except kamma-resultant condition. Mentality is here a condition in other ways, some as a root-cause condition, some as a nutriment condition; and that is in the course of existence, not at rebirth-linking.

Regarding materiality, at rebirth-linking the heart-basis is a condition for consciousness in six ways—as conascence, mutuality, support, dissociation, presence, and non-disappearance conditions. In the course of existence it is a condition in five ways, obtained by omitting the conascence and mutuality conditions (from the previous six) and adding the prenascence condition.

The fivefold materiality classified as the eye-base, etc. is a condition for the corresponding kinds of consciousness, classified as eye-consciousness, etc., in six ways—as support, prenascence, faculty, dissociation, presence, and non-disappearance conditions.

Thus mentality-materiality is a condition for consciousness in many ways.

IT IS TO THIS EXTENT, ĀNANDA, THAT ONE CAN BE BORN ... AND RE-ARISE ...

CY. When consciousness is a condition for mentality-materiality, when mentality-materiality is a condition for consciousness, when the two occur as conditions for one another, it is by this much that one can be born ... pass away and re-arise, that birth, etc., or repeated death and rebirth-linking, can be discerned.

SUB. CY. He shows: "The entire round of saṁsāra occurs by this much—by the five aggregates, here called consciousness and mentality-materiality, occurring with one another as support."

"By this much" (*ettakena*): by this much only. This is a phrase of inclusive emphasis meaning: "not through anything else besides this, through a self having the intrinsic nature of a subject or agent or through a creator God, etc."

TO THIS EXTENT THAT THERE IS A PATHWAY FOR DESIGNATION, ETC.

CY. "A pathway for designation" (*adhivacanapatha*): a pathway for an expression used through the application of a mere word regardless of meaning, as in the case of names such as "Sirivaḍḍhaka," "Dhanavaḍḍhaka," etc. "A pathway for language" (*niruttipatha*): a pathway for an expression used with reference to a reason; thus one is called "mindful" because one has mindfulness or "clearly comprehending" because one clearly comprehends. [504] "A pathway for description" (*paññattipatha*): a pathway for an expression used to communicate (an idea) through diverse aspects; thus "wise, clever, intelligent, subtle, proficient," etc. These three terms refer to the aggregates which become the basis for designation, language, and description.

SUB. CY. "Pathway": a path of application, the domain for its application. Since the terms "designation," "language," and "description" here have the same meaning and all statements share the nature of designation, etc., the words "designation," etc.—though used with distinction (of meaning) in relation to certain statements—here refer to all statements collectively through their sameness in revealing meaning through description.

TO THIS EXTENT THAT THERE IS A SPHERE FOR WISDOM, ETC.

CY. "A sphere for wisdom" (*paññāvacara*): that which is to be encompassed by wisdom, that which can be known. "The round turns": the round of saṁsāra turns. "This present state of being": this is a name for the five aggregates. "For describing": for the sake of describing by names, for the description by the names "feeling," "perception," etc. The meaning is: the five aggregates too are discerned to this extent. "That is, when there is mentality-materiality together with consciousness": what is meant is, to the extent that mentality-materiality and consciousness occur as conditions for one another. This statement refers back (to all previous phrases preceded by "to this extent").

6. Descriptions of Self

23. **CY.** (With the above teaching) the Exalted One has shown the sequel to the phrase "This dependent arising, Ānanda, is deep and appears deep." He now undertakes the present teaching beginning with the ways of describing self in order to show the sequel to the phrase "This generation has become like a tangled skein."

Therein, one who apprehends the unextended kasiṇa sign as self describes self as having material form and as limited. One who gains different kasiṇas sometimes describes it as blue, sometimes as yellow, etc. One who apprehends the extended kasiṇa sign as self describes self as having material form and as infinite. One who removes the unextended kasiṇa sign and apprehends as self either the area that had been covered by the sign or the four mental aggregates occurring there, or, from among these, mere consciousness—he describes self as infinite and immaterial.

SUB. CY. Since no self exists in the ultimate sense, but only as a mental construct of the theorists, the commentator includes the above passage to show what it is they perceive as self and their mental constructions concerning its nature, such as having material form, etc. "Mere consciousness": one who holds the doctrine "the self consists of consciousness."[44]

24. **CY.** "Therein, Ānanda": among these four theorists. "In the present" (*etarahi*): now only, not afterwards. This is said by way of annihilationism. "There in the future" (*tattha bhāviṁ*): there in the world beyond in the future [as ever-existent and imperishable]. This is said by way of eternalism. The third position shows their dispute.[45] For the annihilationist thinks: "The self, which the eternalist posits as not subject to annihilation, is not thus. [505] I will convert him to the way it really is (the state of being thus)—subject to annihilation. I will make him understand his eternalism and cause him to accept annihilationism." The eternalist, too, thinks: "The self, which the annihilationist posits as non-eternal, is not thus. I will convert him to the way it really is (the state of being thus)—eternal. I will make him understand his annihilationism and cause him to accept eternalism."

"This being so": in the case of one describing self as having material form and limited. "A settled view (of self) as having material form and limited underlies this": this view does not underlie this like a vine or creeper; it underlies this in the sense that it has not been abandoned.

SUB. CY. That is, it has not been eradicated by the path. "Underlying" means capable of arising when it gains a cause (which activates it).

CY. To this extent sixteen kinds of theorists have been shown: four who gain meditative attainments, their respective disciples, four rationalists, and their respective disciples.[46]

SUB. CY. The four who gain meditative attainments are the four theorists who describe their doctrinal views after mentally constructing, adopting, and upholding those views themselves as a result of gaining attainments with a material form kasiṇa, etc. Their respective disciples are the four theorists who describe those doctrines after they have learned them from the attainers, either directly or via a lineage of teachers, and then accepted and approved of them in the same way. The four rationalists are the four who, without gaining jhāna through the kasiṇas, adhere to and uphold the four doctrinal views by themselves, entirely as a result of reasoning. Their four disciples should be understood in the way explained.

7. Non-Descriptions of Self

25. **CY.** Having thus shown those who describe self, the Buddha speaks the present section to show those who do not describe self. Who do not describe self? All noble individuals, firstly, do not describe self. Then those who are highly learned—one who is a master of three Piṭakas, two Piṭakas, one Piṭaka, or even the studious expounder of the Dhamma who has thoroughly discriminated one Nikāya, as well as one who has undertaken insight—they do not describe self. They know that the counterpart sign of the kasiṇa is only a counterpart sign and that the immaterial aggregates are only immaterial aggregates.

SUB. CY. "One who has undertaken insight": the power of insight is such that even an unlearned practitioner does not describe self. But this cannot (always) be said for one who gains the jhānas and modes of direct knowledge even though he follows the Buddha's dispensation; thus he is not mentioned here.

"They know that": this is said to show the reason they do not describe self. They do not hold any distorted assumptions because they have dispelled the cause for those assumptions.

8. Considerations of Self

27. Now those who describe self describe it after considering it by way of views, and their consideration comes about because they have not abandoned personality view with its twenty cases. Therefore the Exalted One speaks the present section to show personality view with its twenty cases.

(HE) CONSIDERS FEELING AS SELF …

CY. By this, personality view based on the aggregate of feeling is explained.

"MY SELF IS WITHOUT EXPERIENCE OF FEELING." (*appaṭisaṁvedano me attā*)

CY. This is personality view based on the aggregate of material form.

SUB. CY. By rejecting (self as) a subject of feeling, perceiving and the other mental functions, which are inseparable from feeling, are also rejected. Hence the commentator says "personality view based on the aggregate of material form."

"MY SELF FEELS; FOR MY SELF IS SUBJECT TO FEELING."

CY. This is personality view based on the aggregates of perception, mental formations, and consciousness. [506] For these aggregates feel because they are associated with feeling. The phenomenon of feeling belongs to them and cannot be dissociated from them.

SUB. CY. By the phrase "my self feels" (*attā me vediyati*), the theorist rejects the doctrine that self is without experience of feeling. By the phrase "my self is subject to feeling" (*vedanādhammo hi me attā*), he rejects the doctrine that feeling is self. What he claims is that self is endowed with feeling, that the phenomenon of feeling belongs to self, hence that "self is subject to feeling." "(They) feel because they are associated with feeling": he speaks of them as performing the function (of feeling) through their association with it. For the experiencing of the object pertains to all phenomena taking objects. And that comes about in part merely by being contacted. But feeling, flowing out, experiences the taste of the object as a master. By means of this, perception and the others are said to "feel because they are associated with feeling."

28. THEREIN, ĀNANDA ...

CY. Now the Exalted One shows the errors "therein," in (the doctrines of) the three theorists.

ON THE OCCASION WHEN ONE EXPERIENCES A PLEASANT FEELING, ETC.

CY. The passage beginning with these words is stated in order to show the error (in identifying feeling with self). For whatever feeling one considers as self, it follows that self is sometimes present and sometimes absent.

SUB. CY. Since the three kinds of feeling have different intrinsic natures, one considering pleasant feeling as self cannot consider painful feeling or neither-painful-nor-pleasant feeling as self. The same applies in the other two cases.

29. PLEASANT FEELING IS IMPERMANENT ... SUBJECT TO DESTRUCTION, ETC.

CY. "Impermanent": because of not existing after having been. "Conditioned": made by several causes which have joined together, which have come together. "Dependently arisen": arisen rightly only through a cause, in dependence on several conditions. "Destruction," etc.: all these terms are synonyms for dissolution. For whatever breaks up also is destroyed, falls away, fades out, and ceases.

SUB. CY. "Because of not existing after having been": with this he shows that it is impermanent because of possessing a rise and fall. "Conditioned": because conditioned by numerous causes. "Arisen rightly": arisen through a corresponding cause, an appropriate cause; "rightly," methodically due to the absence of eternalism and annihilationism, etc.; "in dependence on," supported by its own several causes such as a sense faculty, an object, consciousness, a contact to be felt as pleasant, etc. By the four terms—subject to destruction, falling away, fading out, and ceasing—he shows that feeling has the nature of dissolution.

"MY SELF HAS DISAPPEARED" (*byagā me attā*).

CY. The meaning is: "My self has departed, my self has ceased."

Query: Can one and the same person think, at three different times, "This is my self"?

Reply: Why not? For the theorist is not consistent, but wavers like a stump planted in a heap of chaff. Like a monkey in the forest he lets go of one thing and takes hold of another.

SUB. CY. The purport of the question is: "Can one and the same theorist think at three different times, i.e. the times when the three feelings occur, 'This self of mine has pleasant feeling as its intrinsic nature, and also painful feeling and neither-painful-nor-pleasant feeling as its intrinsic nature'? How can anyone in his right mind affirm that one and the same thing can have different intrinsic natures?"

IMPERMANENT, A MIXTURE OF PLEASURE AND PAIN, AND SUBJECT TO ARISING AND FALLING AWAY.

CY. If he makes a distinction and considers a particular kind of feeling to be self, he considers as self something which is impermanent and pleasant, painful, [or neither-painful-nor-pleasant]. If he considers feeling in general to be self, without making distinctions, he considers as self something which is a mixture and subject to arising and falling away. For feeling is threefold and subject to arising and falling away, and the theorist considers that [threefold feeling taken collectively] to be self. Thus he commits the error of accepting an impermanent self and the arising of many feelings at a single moment. But an impermanent self is not allowed and there is no arising of many feelings at a single moment. It is in reference to this that the Exalted One says: "Therefore, Ānanda, because of this it is not acceptable to consider: 'Feeling is my self.'"

SUB. CY. "He commits the error of accepting … the arising of many feelings at a single moment": (because he considers self to have) the intrinsic nature of feeling in general. For if that is so (i.e. that self has the intrinsic nature of feeling in general), the consequence follows that all feelings occur at all times to the self and the theorist would be forced to claim that many feelings arise at a single moment. Not letting him escape, the commentator says: "There is no arising of many feelings at a single moment." The intention is that this is contradicted by direct cognition. "Because of this it is not acceptable": because (this view) has been proven to be self-contradictory and also because self is utterly non-existent, the wise do not accept this view.

30. WHERE THERE IS NOTHING AT ALL THAT IS FELT, COULD (THE IDEA) "I AM" OCCUR THERE?

CY. "Where there is nothing at all that is felt," in the bare aggregate of material form. The meaning is: "Can the ego-conception 'I am' (*asmi*) arise in that which is devoid of feeling, (in a bare material object) such as a palm-leaf fan or a window panel?" Since the bare aggregate of material form does not rise up and say "I am," it is not acceptable (to consider: "My self is without experience of feeling").

31. COULD (THE IDEA) "I AM THIS" OCCUR THERE?

CY. [507] The meaning is: "Among those three aggregates subject to feeling, (if feeling were to cease) would there be even one phenomenon which could be spoken of thus: 'I am this' (*ayam aham asmi*)?" Or else: "When, through the cessation of feeling, those three aggregates have ceased along with feeling, could (the ideas) 'I am' or 'I am this' arise?" The Venerable Ānanda, rejecting this (as untenable) like the sharpness of a hare's horn, says: "Certainly not, venerable sir."

SUB. CY. "I am": this refers to the kind of ego-conception which arises taking the three (other mental) aggregates collectively (to be self). "I am this": this refers to the kind of ego-conception which arises taking one of them individually (to be self). With the cessation of the four mental aggregates there can be no ego-conception; for as with the sharpness of a hare's horn, the supporting base would not be apprehended.

CY. What has been explained so far? The round of existence has been explained. For the Exalted One sometimes explains the round under the heading of ignorance, sometimes under the heading of craving, and sometimes under the heading of views.

Therein, in the passage: "Bhikkhus, no first point of ignorance is discerned, of which it could be said: 'Before this there was no ignorance, afterwards it came into being.' Nevertheless, ignorance has a specific condition" (A.X,61; v,115)—the round is explained under the heading of ignorance. In the passage: "Bhikkhus, no first point of the craving for existence is discerned, of which it could be said: 'Before this there was no craving for existence, afterwards it came into being.' Nevertheless, the craving for existence has a specific condition" (A.X,62; v,116)—the round is explained under the heading of craving. In the passage: "Bhikkhus, no first point of the view of existence is discerned, of which it could be said: 'Before this there was no view of existence, afterwards it came into being.' Nevertheless, the view of existence has a specific condition" (untraced)—the round is explained under the heading of views.

Here, too, the round is explained under the heading of views. For the theorist, having taken pleasant feeling, etc. to be self, misapprehends them through ego-conceptions and conceptions of "mine"; because of this, passing away and re-arising from one state to another in all the realms of existence, modes of origin, destinations, stations for consciousness, and abodes of beings, he continually and constantly revolves like a ship on the ocean driven by a storm, unable to lift his head out from the round.

SUB. CY. Admittedly, in the earlier part of the sutta too (the part on dependent arising), the round of existence was explained. But here, by demonstrating the theorist's inability to lift his head out from the round, the explanation reveals the extremely pernicious nature of wrong view.

"No first point of ignorance is discerned": (the Buddha is saying) "Since a beginning is non-existent, even my unobstructed omniscient knowledge does not discern one, of which it could be said: 'Ignorance arose in the time of such and such a Buddha or universal monarch and did not exist before that time.' " The specific condition for ignorance is the cankers, etc. "Craving for existence" is the craving which becomes the fetter to existence. The "view of existence" is the eternalist view.

32. ĀNANDA, WHEN A BHIKKHU DOES NOT CONSIDER FEELING AS SELF, ETC.

CY. Having so far explained the round in terms of the theorist who is confused about the principle of conditionality, in this section the Exalted One explains the ending of the round. To explain the ending of the round he does not refer to a distracted person who has dropped his meditation subject because of some new work project, etc.; rather, through his skilfulness in teaching, he undertakes the exposition by way of a practitioner dwelling in the foundations of mindfulness. Thus he says: "When a bhikkhu does not consider feeling as self," etc. Such a bhikkhu does not consider feeling or anything else as self because he has proceeded among all phenomena by means of exploration knowledge in the way described thus: "Whatever material form there is—past, present, or future, internal or external, gross or subtle, [508] inferior or superior, far or near—he defines all material form as impermanent; this is one exploration. He defines it as suffering; this is one exploration. He defines it as non-self; this is one exploration," (Pṭs.i., 53) etc. (The same for the other four aggregates).

Not considering in such a way, "he does not cling to anything in the world"; that is, among the phenomena such as material form, etc. belonging to the world of the aggregates, etc., he does not cling to even one thing as self or as belonging to self.

NOT CLINGING, HE IS NOT AGITATED.

CY. He is not agitated (*na paritassati*) by the agitations of craving, views, or conceit. "He personally attains nibbāna": he himself attains nibbāna through the extinguishing of the defilements. "Destroyed is birth," etc.: this is said to show the reviewing knowledge that occurs to one who has attained nibbāna.

ĀNANDA, IF ANYONE SHOULD SAY OF A BHIKKHU WHOSE MIND HAS BEEN THUS LIBERATED, ... THAT WOULD NOT BE PROPER. FOR WHAT REASON?

CY. (Since the arahat does not hold any of the four views concerning the Tathāgata after death) someone might say of him: "The arahat does not know anything." But it would not be correct to say of an arahat, who is liberated through knowledge, that he does not know anything. Thus at the end of the four alternatives it is said: "For what reason?" etc.

BECAUSE THE BHIKKHU IS LIBERATED BY DIRECTLY KNOWING THIS, ETC.

CY. "The extent of designation": "designation" is a term for expression (*vohāra*). "The extent of the pathway for designation": as far as there are aggregates, sense bases, or elements. This method applies to the other cases (i.e. the pathways for language and description). "The sphere for wisdom": the five aggregates, which are to be encompassed by wisdom.

What has been shown so far by the Exalted One? The sequel to the phrase "like a tangled skein" has been shown.

9. The Seven Stations for Consciousness

33. **CY.** Now the person spoken of as "not describing self," as he goes along, eventually becomes one "liberated in both ways." And the person spoken of as "not considering self," as he goes along, eventually becomes one "liberated by wisdom." To show the outcomes and names for these two bhikkhus, the Exalted One undertakes the sections beginning with the one on the seven stations for consciousness.

SUB. CY. (For the one not describing self) the phrase "as he goes along" means that after becoming well-established in the practice of serenity, he goes along by insight and by the path and becomes one liberated in both ways. The one spoken of as "not considering self" is one whose vehicle is insight, and he becomes one liberated by wisdom.

THERE ARE, ĀNANDA, SEVEN STATIONS FOR CONSCIOUSNESS AND TWO BASES.

CY. "Seven" is stated by way of rebirth-linking. "Station for consciousness": this is a foothold for consciousness. [509] "Two bases": two dwelling places, for the word "base" here means a dwelling place. Why is all this included? In order to exhaustively survey the round of existence. For the round is not exhaustively surveyed either by the stations for consciousness alone or by the bases alone, as it is by way of the realms of existence, modes of origin, destinations, and abodes of beings. Therefore all this is included. To analyze the meaning in order he asks: "What are the seven?"

SUB. CY. "Stated by way of rebirth-linking": the seven stations for consciousness are stated by way of rebirth-linking, which is distinguished according to the distinctions of those "who are diverse in body and diverse in perception," etc. For the diversities in body, etc. pertaining to any given order of beings are produced through the rebirth-linking (consciousness) contained in that order, as well as through the accumulation of kamma leading to rebirth there. "A foothold for consciousness": a causal foothold for the present rebirth-linking consciousness. In denotation it is, in five-constituent existence, the four aggregates—

material form, feeling, perception, and mental formations; in four-constituent existence it is the three (mental) aggregates.

BEINGS WHO ARE DIVERSE IN BODY AND DIVERSE IN PERCEPTION, SUCH AS HUMAN BEINGS, SOME GODS, AND SOME BEINGS IN THE LOWER REALMS.

CY. Human beings are mentioned as an example. For among the countless human beings in countless world systems there are not even two who are exactly the same in complexion, figure, etc. Sometimes twins might have the same complexion or figure, but they can still be distinguished by the way they look ahead, look aside, speak, smile, walk, stand, etc. Therefore human beings are said to be "diverse in body." The rebirth-linking perception of humans may be triple-rooted, double-rooted, or rootless; therefore they are said to be "diverse in perception."[47]

"Some gods": the gods of the six sense-sphere heavens. For these may have bodies that are blue, yellow, etc., and their perception may be triple-rooted or double-rooted, though not rootless.

"Some beings in the lower realms": such beings as the female spirits Uttaramātā, Piyaṅkaramātā, Phussamittā, Dhammaguttā, etc., and other spirits who live in places outside the four planes of misery. For their bodies are of diverse colours, shapes, and sizes, and like humans their perception may be double-rooted, triple-rooted, or rootless. But unlike the gods they are not powerful; they are powerless like low-class humans. They have trouble finding food and clothing and live oppressed by pain. Some are afflicted during the dark fortnight and happy during the bright fortnight. Therefore, because they have fallen from the heights of happiness, they are called "beings in the lower realms."[48] Those among them who are triple-rooted can achieve comprehension of the Dhamma. Thus one time at daybreak the female spirit Piyaṅkaramātā heard the Elder Anuruddha reciting the Dhamma and said (to her son Piyaṅkara): [510]

> "Do not make a sound, Piyaṅkara,
> This bhikkhu is reciting passages of Dhamma.
> Perhaps we can learn those passages
> And practise for our true welfare.
>
> "We should refrain from harming beings
> And should not tell conscious lies.
> We should train ourselves in virtue
> To be freed from the goblin realm." (S.X,6; i,209)

Having spoken thus to her little son, she attained the fruit of stream-entry that same day. Uttaramātā became a stream-enterer after hearing the Dhamma from the Exalted One.

BEINGS WHO ARE DIVERSE IN BODY BUT IDENTICAL IN PERCEPTION, SUCH AS THE GODS OF THE BRAHMA-ORDER WHO ARE GENERATED THROUGH THE FIRST (JHĀNA).

CY. "The gods of the Brahma-order" (*devā brahmakāyikā*): the gods of Brahmā's retinue, the gods of Brahmā's ministry, and the great Brahmās.

SUB. CY. Those who occupy the position of attendants to the great Brahmā are gods of Brahmā's retinue; those who occupy the position of the great Brahmā's ministers are gods of Brahmā's ministry; those Brahmās who are great in life-span, beauty, etc. are the great Brahmās.[49]

CY. All these are generated through the first jhāna. Among these, the gods of Brahmā's retinue are generated through a limited (attainment of the first jhāna); their life-span is a third of an aeon. The gods of Brahmā's ministry are generated through a middling (attainment of jhāna); their life-span is half an aeon and their bodies are more pervasive than the gods of Brahmā's retinue. The great Brahmās are generated through a superior (attainment of jhāna); their life-span is an aeon and their bodies are extremely pervasive. Thus, since their bodies are diverse but their perceptions identical by way of the first jhāna, they are described as "beings who are diverse in body but identical in perception."

SUB. CY. A limited (attainment of the first jhāna) is one where the jhāna is merely obtained; a "middling attainment" is one where it is obtained (more firmly) without being well developed; and a "superior attainment" is one where it is well developed and fully mastered.

"More pervasive": larger in size and more beautiful in quality.

"Identical in perception": the identity in their perception is due to its being triple-rooted. For there is no difference at all in that perception by way of associated phenomena.

CY. The beings in the four planes of misery are similar. For these beings are of varying sizes and appearances. Yet for all the (rebirth-linking) perception is a rootless unwholesome resultant. Thus the beings in the planes of misery are also reckoned as "diverse in body but identical in perception."

BEINGS WHO ARE IDENTICAL IN BODY BUT DIVERSE IN PERCEPTION, SUCH AS THE GODS OF STREAMING RADIANCE.

CY. "The gods of streaming radiance" (*devā ābhassarā*): their radiance streams forth from their bodies, flying out after flickering again and again like the flame of a torch.

Those who are reborn as a result of developing the second and third jhānas of the fivefold system to a limited extent become "gods of limited radiance" (*parittābhā*); their life-span is two aeons.[50] Those who are reborn as a result of developing (those jhānas) to a middling extent become "gods of immeasurable radiance" (*appamāṇābhā*); their life-span is four aeons. Those who are reborn as a result of developing (those jhānas) to a superior extent [511] become "gods of streaming radiance"; their life-span is eight aeons. By mentioning the most excellent (of these three planes), all three are included here. For all these gods have bodies that are identical in pervasion; but their perception is diverse in that some have (a rebirth-linking consciousness) without applied thought but with sustained thought, while some have (a rebirth-linking consciousness) without either applied thought or sustained thought.

BEINGS WHO ARE IDENTICAL IN BODY AND IDENTICAL IN PERCEPTION, SUCH AS THE GODS OF REFULGENT BEAUTY.

CY. "The gods of refulgent beauty" (*devā subhakiṇhā*): they are a single mass of beauty, the beauty of their bodily aura. Unlike the gods of streaming radiance, their aura is emitted without flickering. The gods of limited beauty (*parittasubhā*), of immeasurable beauty (*appamāṇasubhā*), and of refulgent beauty are generated into these states by developing the fourth jhāna of the fivefold system to a limited, middling, and superior extent, respectively; their respective life-spans are sixteen, thirty-two, and sixty-four aeons. Thus they are "identical in body" and also, through the perception pertaining to the fourth jhāna (as a rebirth-linking consciousness), "identical in perception."

The gods of abundant fruit (*vehapphalā*) are also assigned to the fourth station for consciousness. The non-percipient beings, not having consciousness, are not included here, but they are included among the abodes of beings. The gods of the pure abodes, pertaining to the ending of the round, do not always exist. They do not arise in the world when it is devoid of Buddhas even for 100,000 aeons or for an incalculable period. They arise only when Buddhas have arisen, during a period of 16,000 aeons. These planes are like a special camp-ground of the Exalted One, after he has set in motion the wheel of Dhamma; thus they are not assigned to either the stations for consciousness or the abodes of beings. The meaning of the other stations is explained in the *Visuddhimagga*.[51] The base of neither perception nor non-perception is included among the bases but not among the stations for consciousness; for like perception this consciousness is so subtle that it is called "neither consciousness nor non-consciousness."

SUB. CY. "So subtle": since it has attained the subtlety of residual formations.[52] It is "not consciousness" because it lacks the distinctive function of consciousness and "not non-consciousness" because it is not completely non-consciousness. Therefore it is not included among the stations for consciousness, where the distinctive function of consciousness is in evidence.

34. THEREIN, ĀNANDA, IF ONE UNDERSTANDS THE FIRST STATION FOR CONSCIOUSNESS, ETC.

CY. "Its origin": one understands its origin by the method, "through the origination of ignorance material form originates," etc. "Its passing away": [512] one understands its passing away by the method, "through the cessation of ignorance material form ceases," etc. (Pṭs. i,55f.).[53]

"Its satisfaction": one understands its satisfaction thus: "The pleasure and joy that arise in dependence on material form … consciousness: this is the satisfaction in consciousness." "Its unsatisfactoriness": one understands its unsatisfactoriness thus: "That material form … consciousness is impermanent, suffering, and subject to change: this is the unsatisfactoriness in consciousness." "The escape from it": one understands the escape from it thus: "The removal and abandoning of desire and lust for material form … consciousness: this is the escape from consciousness" (S.XXII,26; iii,28).

This method of interpretation should be applied to all the other stations for consciousness. But where there is no material form (i.e. in the immaterial planes) the origin should be interpreted by way of the four mental aggregates only; and where there is no consciousness (i.e. among non-percipient beings) it should be interpreted by way of the one aggregate (of material form). Thus here the passage should be interpreted with the phrases "through the origination of nutriment" and "through the cessation of nutriment."

IS IT PROPER FOR ONE TO SEEK ENJOYMENT IN IT?

CY. Is it right for that bhikkhu to seek enjoyment in that station for consciousness as "I" or "mine" by way of craving, conceit, or views?

SUB. CY. Seeking enjoyment as "I" occurs by way of conceit and views, as "mine" by way of craving.

ĀNANDA, WHEN A BHIKKHU ... IS LIBERATED THROUGH NON-CLINGING, THEN HE IS CALLED A BHIKKHU LIBERATED BY WISDOM.

CY. He is liberated by not grasping anything through the four kinds of clinging. "Liberated by wisdom": having brought about the [future] non-occurrence of the mental body and the material body, he is liberated solely by the power of wisdom without realizing the eight emancipations. This type is fivefold: the dry-insight meditator and those who attain arahatship after having become established in one or another of the four jhānas. It is said: "Who is the individual liberated by wisdom? Herein, some individual does not dwell suffusing the eight emancipations with the body; but having seen with wisdom, his cankers are destroyed. This individual is called 'one liberated by wisdom' " (Pug., pp. 14, 73).

SUB. CY. "Liberated by wisdom": he is liberated solely by the power of wisdom because he does not achieve the eight emancipations and thus lacks the power of eminent concentration. Or else, "liberated by wisdom" means liberated while understanding; that is, knowing and penetrating the four truths in the modes of full understanding, etc. without contact with the first jhāna,[54] he is "liberated" or distinctively freed by completing the functions (of penetration) by bringing those functions to their climax.

"Dry-insight meditator": one whose insight is dry, rough, and unmoistened, lacking the moisture of serenity meditation.

"Does not dwell suffusing the eight emancipations": this indicates the absence of the power of eminent concentration. "Having seen with wisdom": this indicates possession of the power of eminent wisdom.

10. The Eight Emancipations

35. **CY.** Having thus shown the outcome and name for the first bhikkhu, the Exalted One explains the eight emancipations in order to show the outcome and name for the other one.

SUB. CY. For the first bhikkhu, the outcome occurs through full understanding, etc. of the seven stations for consciousness, etc.; thus his name is "liberated by wisdom." The other is the one liberated in both ways.

ĀNANDA THERE ARE THESE EIGHT EMANCIPATIONS (*aṭṭha vimokkhā*).

CY. In what sense are they emancipations? In the sense of releasing (*adhimuccana*). And in what sense are they releasing? In the sense of freeing thoroughly from the adverse phenomena and in the sense of freeing thoroughly by way of delight in the object. What is meant is: (the mind's) occurrence on the object without constraint, free from apprehension, similar to the way a little boy sleeps in his father's lap, his body completely relaxed. But the latter meaning [513] applies only to the first seven emancipations, not to the last one.[55]

SUB. CY. "In the sense of releasing": the word "releasing" signifies the distinguished development of any fine-material-sphere jhāna to the degree that liberation from opposing states takes place by the suppression (of defilements) and the jhāna occurs eminently, liberated from the opposing states by means of that distinguished development. For though there is sameness in kind (between individual jhāna attainments), through distinguished development there is also a distinction in the quality of their occurrence. Thus "emancipation" has the meaning of releasing thoroughly by way of liberation from adverse mental phenomena and by way of delight (in the object) without constraint, free from apprehension.[56] The last emancipation is cessation. The meaning solely of being liberated (from adverse phenomena) obtains there, as the commentator himself says.

ONE POSSESSING MATERIAL FORM SEES MATERIAL FORMS.

CY. Here, the material form (possessed) is the fine-material-sphere jhāna aroused through a blue kasiṇa, etc., using as the blue kasiṇa, etc. something internal such as the hairs of the head, etc. One having that material form is "one possessing material form" (*rūpī*).

SUB. CY. "Possessing material form" means endowed with the material form included in one's own continuity that is distinguished as the cause for the jhāna; because of that material form one is spoken of as "one possessing material form." Since this phrase signifies a special meaning, it should be understood that the jhāna obtained through the material form included in one's own continuity is itself the referent here, in the ultimate sense, of the state of "possessing material form."

CY. "(One) sees material forms": with the eye of jhāna one also sees material forms such as the blue kasiṇa, etc. externally. By this (first emancipation) the four fine-material-sphere jhānas are shown for a person who arouses jhāna through the kasiṇas based on internal objects.

ONE NOT PERCEIVING MATERIAL FORMS INTERNALLY SEES MATERIAL FORMS EXTERNALLY.

CY. This means that he does not arouse the fine-material-sphere jhānas on his own head hairs, etc. By this the fine-material-sphere jhānas are shown for someone who does the preparatory work externally and arouses jhānas only externally.

ONE IS RELEASED UPON THE IDEA OF THE BEAUTIFUL.

CY. By this are shown the jhānas attained through very pure colour kasiṇas. In the meditative absorption itself there is no concern with the idea of the beautiful. But because one who dwells in meditation taking as his object a pure and beautiful kasiṇa can be described as "released upon the idea of the beautiful," the teaching is expounded in those words.

In the *Paṭisambhidāmagga*, however, it is said: " 'One is released upon the idea of the beautiful'—how is this an emancipation? Herein, a bhikkhu dwells pervading one direction, etc. with a mind endowed with loving-kindness; through the development of loving-kindness beings are not repulsive to him. So too for compassion, sympathetic joy, and equanimity. Such is the emancipation: 'One is released upon the idea of the beautiful' " (Pṭs.ii,39).

SUB. CY. For practitioners who take very pure colour kasiṇas as their object of meditation, emancipation in the sense of "releasing thoroughly" occurs by way of delight; therefore the commentator explains the third emancipation in this way. But since the meditative development occurring by way of loving-kindness, promoting non-repulsion towards beings, releases one from repulsion towards them, the *Paṭisambhidāmagga* says: "The development of the divine dwellings (*brahmavihāra*) is the emancipation of the beautiful." Either explanation may be recognized, since in the way they are stated there is no contradiction between them.

CY. Everything that has to be said about the immaterial emancipations has already been said in the *Visuddhimagga* (Chapter X, XXIII). The eighth emancipation is the highest emancipation, since it is completely purified and liberated from the four (mental) aggregates.

SUB. CY. It is "the highest emancipation" because it can be attained only by noble ones and because it qualifies as the attainment of "nibbāna here and now," since it terminates in the noble fruit.

36. ĀNANDA, WHEN A BHIKKHU ATTAINS THESE EIGHT EMANCIPATIONS IN FORWARD ORDER, ETC. ... THEN HE IS CALLED A BHIKKHU WHO IS LIBERATED IN BOTH WAYS.

CY. "In forward order": from the beginning to the end. "In reverse order": from the end back to the beginning. "In both forward and reverse order": this is said with reference to his cruising back and forth through the attainments without stopping (in any one attainment), a result of his great proficiency.

"Whenever he wants" (*yatthicchakaṁ*) signifies place: in whatever place he wishes. "In whatever way he wants" (*yadicchakaṁ*) signifies the attainment: whichever attainment he wishes. "As long as he wants" (*yāvaticchakaṁ*) signifies the length of time: for as long a period of time as he wishes. [514]

"Liberated in both ways" (*ubhatobhāgavimutta*): liberated through two portions and liberated from two portions.[57] Through the immaterial attainments he is liberated from the material body and through the path he is liberated from the mental body. It is said:

> "As a flame struck by a gust of wind
> (Upasīva," the Exalted One said,)
> "Reaches its end and can be reckoned no more,
> So the sage liberated from the mental body
> Reaches his end and can be reckoned no more." (Sn. v.1074)

SUB. CY. "Liberated through two portions and liberated from two portions": he is liberated through the two liberating portions (*vimuccanabhāgehi*), i.e. through the emancipation by suppression effected by the immaterial jhāna and through the emancipation by eradication effected by the path. And he is also liberated from the two portions one should be liberated from (*vimuccitabbabhāgehi*), i.e. from the material body through the immaterial attainment and from the mental body through the path. "Liberated" means liberated from defilements. Thus the meaning here is: being liberated, he has been liberated from the two bodies by the suppression and eradication of defilements.

In the verse addressed to the brahmin Upasīva, a gainer of the base of nothingness, the Exalted One referred to one liberated in both ways as "the sage liberated from the mental body." The sage (*muni*), here a learner (*sekha*) reborn in the immaterial realm, has by the nature (of his rebirth) already been liberated from the material body. There he produces the fourth path and, by fully understanding the mental body, he

Can be reckoned no more.

becomes liberated from the mental body as well. Having become a cankerless arahat liberated in both ways, he "reaches his end," final nibbāna without clinging, "and can be reckoned no more," he cannot be designated anymore as a warrior, a brahmin, etc.

CY. The "one liberated in both ways" is fivefold: those who attain arahatship after emerging from one or another of the immaterial attainments, and the one who, having been a non-returner, attains arahatship after emerging from cessation.

SUB. CY. *Query*: When it is said "after emerging from one or another of the immaterial attainments," does this refer to someone who attains any one of them or to someone who attains all the immaterial states?

Reply: You can understand it in either way, as you like. If it is stated by way of one who attains all the immaterial states, there is no contradiction.

Query: But if it is taken to mean someone who attains only one of them, would that not be contradicted by the statement in the sutta: "When a bhikkhu attains these eight emancipations," etc.?

Reply: Someone who gains even one immaterial-sphere jhāna is called a gainer of the eight emancipations, since it is possible to apply the name "eight emancipations" even to a single part of the set. For this designation "eight emancipations" can be attributed to a single part of the set just as well as to the whole. Thus it is said: "after emerging from one or another of the immaterial attainments."

CY. Some say: "Since the fourth fine-material-sphere jhāna has two factors and is associated with equanimity, it is just like an immaterial jhāna. Therefore one who attains arahatship after emerging from the fourth fine-material-sphere jhāna is also liberated in both ways."

SUB. CY. Some imagine that the one liberated in both ways can be sixfold; that is merely their opinion. The phrase "some say" shows that this issue has been decided by the ancient teachers.[58] The "some" are the residents of the Uttaravihāra and the teachers of the *Sārasamāsa*. For they say "liberated in both ways" means liberated by both ways (*ubhayabhāgavimutta*), that is, liberated through concentration and insight; and they think liberation from the obstacles to concentration also comes about through concentration of the fine-material sphere. Thus in the *Sārasamāsa* it is said: "Liberated by both, i.e. by a portion of the fine-material-sphere jhānas and by a portion of the immaterial jhānas."

CY. This question of the one liberated in both ways was raised in the Bronze Palace (of the Mahāvihāra) and a decision was reached after a long time in reliance upon the explanation of the Elder Tipiṭaka

Cūḷa Sumana. In the Giri Vihāra, it is said, a pupil of the Elder heard the question from the mouth of an alms-wandering monk and said: "Friend, before our teacher explained this matter in the Bronze Palace, no one knew the answer."

"What did the Elder say, venerable sir?"

"He said that even though the fourth jhāna of the fine-material-sphere has two factors, is accompanied by equanimity, and suppresses the defilements, it still operates in proximate range to the defilements, in the field for their growth. For in five-constituent existence the defilements assail the mind with the decisive support of a (sensory) object, such as the colour blue, etc., and the fine-material-sphere jhāna does not surmount such objects.[59] Therefore 'liberated in both ways' signifies one who attains arahatship after completely turning away from material form and suppressing the defilements by means of an immaterial jhāna."

Having said this he quoted the sutta: "Who is the individual liberated in both ways? Herein, some individual dwells suffusing the eight emancipations with the body, [515] and having seen with wisdom, his cankers are destroyed. This individual is called one liberated in both ways" (Pug., pp. 14, 73).

SUB. CY. (An immaterial attainment is necessary to be "liberated in both ways" since) the development of the immaterial attainments suppresses the defilements more effectively than the development of the fine-material jhānas, for the former marks the development of the fading out of the material and represents a higher stage of development.

The best of all "liberations in both ways" should be understood as the liberation attained when one has prepared the mental continuum extremely well by attaining the eight emancipations in forward order, etc., then takes the eighth and highest emancipation as a basis, arouses insight, and achieves the supreme path.

The Commentary to the Mahānidāna Sutta is concluded.

TABLE 2

THE SEVEN STATIONS FOR CONSCIOUSNESS AND THE TWO BASES

IMMATERIAL REALM	Base only	Base of neither perception nor non-perception
	7th Station for Consciousness	Base of nothingness
	6th Station for Consciousness	Base of infinity of consciousness
	5th Station for Consciousness	Base of infinity of space
FINE-MATERIAL REALM	Base only	Base of non-percipient beings
	4th Station for Consciousness: beings identical in body, identical in perception	Gods of abundant fruit Gods of refulgent beauty Gods of immeasurable beauty
	3rd Station for Consciousness: beings identical in body, diverse in perception	Gods of streaming radiance Gods of immeasurable radiance Gods of limited radiance
	2nd Station for Consciousness: beings diverse in body, identical in perception	Great Brahmās Gods of Brahmā's ministry Gods of Brahmā's retinue
SENSE-SPHERE REALM	1st Station for Consciousness: beings diverse in body, diverse in perception	Sense-sphere gods Human beings Some beings in the lower worlds
	2nd Station for Consciousness beings diverse in body, identical in perception (plane of misery)	Host of titans (*asura*) Realm of afflicted spirits (*peta*) Animal realm Hells

APPENDIX

CONDITIONAL RELATIONS AND DEPENDENT ARISING

One of the major projects undertaken in the Pali commentaries is the interpretation of the teachings found in the Sutta Piṭaka with the aid of the highly refined classificatory system delineated in the Abhidhamma Piṭaka. The Abhidhamma system is distinguished by two complementary methods in the treatment of experience: (i) a precise analysis of experience into momentary phenomena regarded as the fundamental constituents of actuality; and (ii) the correlation of these phenomena through a scheme of twenty-four conditional relations. The first is the special province of the *Dhammasaṅgaṇī*, the first book of the Abhidhamma Piṭaka; the second, of the *Paṭṭhāna*, the seventh and final book. The basic categories used to classify the phenomena discovered through analysis are three: states of consciousness (*citta*), the mental factors (*cetasika*) which enter into association with them, and the material phenomena (*rūpa*) which serve as their bases, objects, and general supports. Besides these, an unconditioned element is recognized, *nibbāna*, which is not momentary and not arisen through conditions.

To explicate the Suttanta teachings by means of the Abhidhamma method, the commentaries translate their freer, more discursive and personalistic expositions into the technical Abhidhamma language of "bare phenomena" (*suddhadhammā*) linked together by nothing more personal than laws of conditional relatedness. The Suttanta statement of dependent arising already exhibits certain essential features of the Abhidhamma approach and thus does not require radical reformulation. In fact, it even provides the material for an entire chapter of the *Vibhaṅga* (Chapter VI), which treats it both from the Suttanta standpoint and by way of the analytical Abhidhamma method. The *Paṭṭhāna* itself does not subject the formula for dependent arising to its own system of relations; but the commentaries, ever aiming at maximum precision in their exegesis of sutta formulations, apply the method to the connection between each pair of factors, elucidating it by way of the relevant relations.

The application is fully worked out for the standard twelvefold formula for dependent arising in the *Visuddhimagga*, which prefaces its account with an explanation of the twenty-four conditions. As the commentary to the Mahānidāna Sutta assumes that its reader has this work at hand, it treats the connections only in a summary way, expanded but not explained in the subcommentary. Hence, to aid the reader unfamiliar with the method, this supplementary section has been appended briefly explaining the twenty-four conditional relations and illustrating their application to dependent arising in the exegetical texts.

The System of Relations

The Pali word being translated "conditional relation" is the same as that translated as "condition"—*paccaya*. But what is intended by the former use of the word are the specific modalities in which certain things, the conditioning phenomena (*paccaya-dhammā*), function as conditions for other things, the conditionally arisen phenomena (*paccay' uppannā dhammā*). A distinction in modalities is already implicit in the Suttanta account of conditionality, which shows phenomena of quite different kinds contributing in quite different ways to the arising of a single dependent state. The *Paṭṭhāna* enumerates the variety of conditional modes in minute detail, exploring every nook and corner of the inter-connections. Its elaboration of twenty-four conditional relations may represent a later stage of thought than the account found in the suttas; but it is fully consistent with this account, and by exhibiting the diverse ways in which the conditioning function can be exercised, it reveals the vast range of the Suttanta principle and prevents simplistic reductionism in interpreting it.

Though the exegetical texts do not bring all twenty-four conditions into connection with the teaching of dependent arising, for the sake of completeness the entire set has been listed. Limitations of space and aim require that the explanations be kept brief. Fuller explanations of dependent arising by way of the *Paṭṭhāna* system can be found in the *Visuddhimagga* (Chapter XVII) and in the works of Venerable Nyanatiloka referred to under "Texts Used."

The Twenty-four Conditional Relations

1. Root-cause condition (*hetupaccaya*)
2. Object condition (*ārammaṇapaccaya*)
3. Predominance condition (*adhipatipaccaya*)
4. Proximity condition (*anantarapaccaya*)

5. Contiguity condition (*samanantarapaccaya*)
6. Conascence condition (*sahajātapaccaya*)
7. Mutuality condition (*aññamaññapaccaya*)
8. Support condition (*nissayapaccaya*)
9. Decisive support condition (*upanissayapaccaya*)
10. Prenascence condition (*purejātapaccaya*)
11. Postnascence condition (*pacchājātapaccaya*)
12. Repetition condition (*āsevanapaccaya*)
13. Kamma condition (*kammapaccaya*)
14. Kamma-result condition (*vipākapaccaya*)
15. Nutriment condition (*āhārapaccaya*)
16. Faculty condition (*indriyapaccaya*)
17. Jhāna condition (*jhānapaccaya*)
18. Path condition (*maggapaccaya*)
19. Association condition (*sampayuttapaccaya*)
20. Dissociation condition (*vippayuttapaccaya*)
21. Presence condition (*atthipaccaya*)
22. Absence condition (*natthipaccaya*)
23. Disappearance condition (*vigatapaccaya*)
24. Non-disappearance condition (*avigatapaccaya*)

(1) Root-cause condition refers to six mental factors called roots (*mūla, hetu*) because they give strength and stability to the phenomena they condition in the same way that the roots of a tree give strength and stability to the tree. Three roots—greed, hatred, and delusion—are exclusively unwholesome. The other three—non-greed, non-hatred, and non-delusion—are wholesome when they arise in wholesome states of consciousness and ethically indeterminate (*abyākata*) when they arise in resultant states and in the functional consciousness of an arahat. Phenomena that are root-cause conditions function as conditions for the mental phenomena associated with themselves (states of consciousness and other mental factors) and for the material phenomena originated by the state of consciousness to which they belong.

(2) An *object condition* is a phenomenon that serves as a condition for consciousness and its associated mental factors by being taken as their object. The object condition is sixfold as visible form, sound, smell, taste, tactile object, and purely mental object.

(3) *Predominance condition* is of two kinds, object and conascent. An object predominance condition is any object given special importance by the mind. A conascent predominance condition is one of four factors—desire (to achieve), energy, consciousness, and investigation—

which takes on a dominant role in directing the state of consciousness to which it belongs. In any single state of consciousness only one of the four can assume such a role.

(4) & (5) The *proximity* and *contiguity conditions* are identical in meaning. They both refer to any state of consciousness and its mental factors in so far as they are capable of arousing the state of consciousness and its mental factors that follow them immediately in the continuum of consciousness.

(6) A *conascence condition* is a phenomenon that, in arising, makes other phenomena arise together with itself, similar to the way a lamp causes light to come forth as soon as it is turned on.

(7) A *mutuality condition* is a phenomenon that assists another by means of mutual arousing and stabilization, similar to the way the three legs of a tripod enable each other to stand. The mutuality relationship is a specific type of conascence, so that all phenomena functioning as mutuality conditions also function as conascence conditions. Thus in any given state of consciousness, all the mental phenomena are both conascence and mutuality conditions for all the others. The same holds for each of the four primary material elements in relation to the others, and for mental and material phenomena in relation to each other at the moment of rebirth-linking. However, the two modes of conditionality are not co-extensive: there are cases of conascence which exclude mutuality. These are: mental phenomena in relation to material phenomena originated by consciousness, and the four primary material elements in relation to derived materiality. Here, though there is simultaneity in arising, the relationship is not symmetrical. The former member of each pair exercises a conditional efficacy towards the latter which is not reciprocated by the latter towards itself.

(8) A s*upport condition* is a phenomenon that assists other phenomena by serving as a foundation for them; thus it is said to support them in the way the earth supports trees or a canvas supports a painting. This condition encompasses the conascence relationship, so that all conascent conditions are also support conditions for their conditionally arisen phenomena. But the support condition has a wider range than conascence and applies to some phenomena which do not share a simultaneous origination with the states they arouse, but momentarily precede them. Thus the five internal sense bases are support conditions in this way for their respective kinds of sense consciousness together with their mental factors. So too is the heart-basis for the states of consciousness and mental factors that take it as their organic base during the course of existence (at rebirth it is a conascent support condition).

(9) A *decisive support condition* is a phenomenon that assists another by serving as a strong cause for its arising. This kind of condition is threefold as object decisive support, proximity decisive support, and natural decisive support. The first is identical in denotation with object predominance condition, the second with proximity condition; the different classifications are made merely to accentuate different aspects of the conditioning function without implying an actual difference in the relationship itself. The third kind, natural decisive support, signifies anything which naturally becomes a strong cause for the arising of other phenomena. Thus hatred may be a natural decisive support for murder, greed for theft, faith for engaging in charity, meditation for the growth of wisdom.

(10) A *prenascence condition* is a phenomenon that arises earlier than another and assists the latter to arise by remaining present after it has itself already arisen. Thus the five sense objects and the five internal sense bases are prenascence conditions for their respective kinds of consciousness and mental factors, the heart-basis for the states of consciousness and mental factors that take it as their organic base during the course of existence.

(11) *Postnascence condition* refers to states of consciousness and their mental factors insofar as they function as a condition for the preservation and strengthening of the previously arisen body.

(12) *Repetition condition* refers to phenomena that assist and strengthen succeeding phenomena through the power of repetition. This condition applies only to wholesome, unwholesome, and functional indeterminate mental phenomena when they serve as condition for immediately succeeding mental phenomena having the same ethical quality as themselves. In the technical vocabulary of Abhidhamma thought, this conditional function is exercised by each *javana* moment in relation to the succeeding *javana* moment in a single process of consciousness (*cittavīthi*).

(13) *Kamma condition* is twofold. First, wholesome and unwholesome volition is a kamma condition for resultant mental phenomena and for material phenomena produced through kamma. Second, conascent volition is a kamma condition for its associated mental phenomena and for the material phenomena originated by the states of consciousness to which it belongs.

(14) *Kamma-result condition* refers to mental phenomena resulting from past kamma in relation to each other and to certain kinds of material phenomena.

(15) *Nutriment condition* refers to four factors, called nutriments

because they "nourish" the psychophysical organism: material food, contact, volition, and consciousness. Material food is a nutriment condition for the physical body, the other three for their associated mental phenomena and for material phenomena originated by consciousness.

(16) *Faculty condition* applies to twenty mental and material phenomena designated as faculties because they dominate and direct the states that come under their influence. Thus, for example, the five physical sense faculties serve as faculty condition for the mental phenomena that originate through them, the mind faculty and the five spiritual faculties—faith, energy, mindfulness, concentration, and wisdom—for their associated mental phenomena and for material phenomena originated by consciousness.

(17) *Jhāna condition* refers to seven mental phenomena called jhāna factors in the sense that they intensify and concentrate the state of consciousness to which they belong.

(18) *Path condition* refers to twelve mental phenomena called path factors in the sense that they provide an escape from various situations and lead to different destinations. The most prominent of these are the eight factors of the noble eightfold path leading to the cessation of suffering.

(19) *Association condition* applies to conascent mental phenomena, which assist each other through their association by having a common physical base, a common object, and a simultaneous arising and cessation.

(20) *Dissociation condition* applies to material phenomena that assist mental phenomena, and mental phenomena that assist material phenomena, by way of the essential differences between the two kinds of states. It is threefold as comprising prenascent, postnascent, and conascent phenomena.

(21) *Presence condition* refers to a phenomenon that serves as a condition for other phenomena through its presence alongside the latter. It includes conditions 6, 7, 8, 10 and 11, as well as others on particular occasions that call them into relevance.

(22) *Absence condition* refers to mental phenomena which, by their ceasing, enable the mental phenomena immediately following themselves to arise. This condition is identical in denotation with conditions 4 and 5.

(23) *Disappearance condition* is identical with condition 22.

(24) *Non-disappearance condition* is identical with condition 21.

The Method Applied

To illustrate how the modes of conditionality are applied to dependent arising, several propositions within the formula may be taken for consideration. We will start with the statement: "With consciousness as condition there is mentality-materiality."

At "rebirth-linking," i.e. the moment of conception, the rebirth-consciousness arises together with its associated mental factors, both being supported by the newly fertilized ovum. This cell consists of a variety of material phenomena, the most important of which is the heart-basis. Since consciousness and the other mental phenomena, which belong to "mentality," arise and cease simultaneously, consciousness is a condition for mentality as conascence, support, association, presence, and non-disappearance conditions. Since, as conascents, their conditional efficacy is reciprocal, it is also related to them as a mutuality condition, and as kamma-result condition because they all result from the same previous kamma responsible for generating rebirth. As the fourth nutriment, consciousness is a nutriment condition for its associated mental factors, and as the mind faculty it is a faculty condition for them. In these ways the nine conditions stated in the subcommentary are obtained. On any occasion of resultant consciousness following rebirth-linking, consciousness is a condition for associated mentality in the same nine ways.

In relation to materiality, the subcommentary says that at rebirth, consciousness is a condition for the materiality of the heart-basis in nine ways. Eight of these are identical with the aforementioned ways in which consciousness is a condition for mentality, the one difference being the substitution of dissociation condition for association condition. This change is made necessary by the definition of the latter as applying only to conascent mental phenomena and of the former as applying only to co-existent mental and material phenomena. For the other kinds of materiality arising at the moment of conception, the rebirth-consciousness is a condition in all the above ways except mutuality; for though they are conascent, their conditional efficacy with regard to each other is not fully reciprocal. The kammically active consciousness of the previous life responsible for the present rebirth is a condition for the materiality produced by kamma only in one way, as a natural decisive support condition.

A second example that can be examined is the converse: "With mentality-materiality as condition there is consciousness"; thus we subject both arms of the "hidden vortex" to analysis. The subcommentary mentions seven general ways in which, at rebirth, mentality is a condition for consciousness; these can easily be understood from the previous explanation, for they simply reverse the relations shown above. Besides these, particular mental factors can function as a condition for consciousness in other ways. The subcommentary mentions only two, root-cause and nutriment conditions, but the outline given in the *Paṭṭhāna* indicates that the faculty, jhāna, and path conditions could also have been brought in. During the course of existence following rebirth, resultant mentality is a condition for resultant consciousness in the same seven invariable ways and by way of various additional conditions depending on the occasion.

Next to be considered is the conditionality for consciousness of non-resultant mentality, that is, the mental factors occurring in kammically active and in functional states of mind. Non-resultant mentality, the subcommentary says, is a condition for the associated consciousness in six general ways: in all the ways mentioned above except kamma-result condition, which obviously must be excluded. But particular mental phenomena can function as conditions for consciousness in more specialized ways, such as root-cause, faculty, jhāna, and path conditions.

Material phenomena also serve as a condition for consciousness. The subcommentary begins with the heart-basis, mentioning six ways it serves as a condition for consciousness at rebirth: conascence, mutuality, support, dissociation, presence, and non-disappearance. It is a conascence condition (and therefore also a presence and non-disappearance condition) because the heart-basis and consciousness spring into existence at the same moment of rebirth-linking; a support condition because it serves as the material foundation for the rebirth-consciousness; and a mutuality condition because the two are conascents with reciprocal conditional efficiency. During the course of existence the heart-basis arises, not simultaneously with consciousness as at rebirth, but a brief moment earlier. Thus the conascence and mutuality relations cease, while the heart-basis becomes a prenascence condition for the states of consciousness it supports. The relations of support, dissociation, presence, and non-disappearance, however, continue. Thus, during life, the heart-basis is a condition for consciousness in five ways.

During the course of existence, the five physical sense faculties can become conditions for consciousness. Each is a condition for its respective kind of sense consciousness in the six ways mentioned in the subcommentary; these can easily be understood by consulting the schedule of the conditions. The subcommentary does not mention the five kinds of sense objects, but these can serve as a condition for their respective kinds of consciousness in at least five ways: as object, prenascence, dissociation, presence, and non-disappearance conditions. Some objects, given special prominence, can also become object predominance and object decisive support conditions.

One final example illustrating a different aspect of conditionality is the statement: "With clinging as condition there is existence." The commentary says that clinging is a condition for existence under the headings of both decisive support and conascence. As we saw, "existence" is explained by the commentators as the kamma leading to renewed existence, and kamma is identified as mundane wholesome and unwholesome volition. Clinging, in turn, is equated with two mental factors: clinging to sense pleasures with greed, the other three kinds of clinging with views. Thus the original sutta statement, reformulated in terms of specific mental factors entering into the Abhidhamma system, expresses the conditionality of sensual greed and views for the volitions they arouse and influence. Volition must be present on any occasion of greed or views, and as mental factors they must arise simultaneously; thus clinging is a condition for existence as a conascence condition. The subcommentary explains that, as a "heading," conascence here includes along with itself the mutuality, support, association, presence, and non-disappearance conditions. Since greed and views are unwholesome mental factors, they pass on their unwholesomeness to their conascent volition. Thus the kamma generated simultaneously with the arising of clinging is necessarily unwholesome. This holds whether the volition expresses itself in bodily or verbal action or remains unexpressed as bare mental action.

In any of its four forms, clinging can also function as a condition for kamma following it after an interval of time. It then becomes a decisive support condition for existence. As a natural decisive support condition for volition occurring at a later time, clinging can motivate volition with an ethical quality opposite to its own; that is, the unwholesome greed and views comprised under clinging can induce wholesome kamma leading to favourable forms of rebirth. For example, someone strongly attached to sense pleasures might hear that the heavenly worlds offer greater sensual enjoyment than the human world. Instructed that charity and moral conduct are the means to a heavenly rebirth, he might then become exceedingly generous and very pure in his observance of morality, even to the point of developing an abstemious attitude towards sense enjoyment in this life. Thus his clinging to sense pleasures, transferred to a celestial afterlife, functions as a condition for him to undertake wholesome actions leading to rebirth in the sense-sphere heavens.

Again, someone might adopt the wrong view that existence in the fine-material or immaterial realms is everlasting. Yearning for eternal life, he then develops the jhānas and immaterial attainments conducive to rebirth into those realms. In this case a wrong eternalist view becomes the condition for the wholesome kamma generated in achieving the higher meditative attainments. Or someone might come to believe that merely by undertaking precepts and practising certain austerities he can gain full deliverance from suffering. In the hope of such deliverance, he takes up rules of conduct enjoining harmlessness and restraint, and observes such austere practices as celibacy, moderation in eating, and fewness of wants. Though his view is wrong, a case of "clinging to rules and observances," it induces him to engage in wholesome actions. Thereby he generates kamma which will bring him pleasant fruits even if it fails to yield the complete deliverance he expects. Still again, a person might adopt the doctrine that the jhānas and immaterial attainments bring the realization of the true self. Through his clinging to a doctrine of self, he cultivates these attainments, as a consequence of which he takes rebirth in a fine-material or immaterial realm of existence.

From these examples it can be seen that clinging, though an unwholesome factor in itself, is capable of motivating wholesome kamma-existence leading to higher forms of rebirth-existence. However, the states of existence to which clinging leads are all impermanent, incapable of giving full security from suffering, and inherently liable to pass away. Thus the Buddha teaches that to attain deliverance from suffering, clinging in all its forms must be eradicated.

NOTES

INTRODUCTION

1. *Imasmiṁ sati idaṁ hoti; imass' uppādā idaṁ uppajjati. Imasmiṁ asati idaṁ na hoti; imassa nirodhā idaṁ nirujjhati* (e.g. S.XII,21; ii,28).
2. It will be noted that, as the twelvefold formula accounts for the origin and cessation of suffering, it offers an expanded version of the second and third noble truths. In fact, in one sutta (A.III,61; i,177) the two sides of the formula are stated in full as explanations of these two truths.
3. For a tabular comparison of the two versions, see Table 1.
4. The two words *attha* and *dhamma* have been rendered here as "meaning" and "phenomena" for the sake of consistency with the rest of the translation and because that seems to be their intended literal meaning. Puzzlement may arise over the connection between the commentary's explanations of the two "depths" and the terms "meaning" and "phenomena." The key to this connection is found in the *Visuddhimagga* (XIV, 22-23), which in elucidating the two terms *atthapaṭisambhidā*, "analytical knowledge of meaning," and *dhammapaṭisambhidā*, "analytical knowledge of phenomena," explains *attha* as a term for the effect of a cause (*hetuphala*) and *dhamma* as a condition (*paccaya*). In support of this interpretation, the commentator quotes the *Vibhaṅga* (of the Abhidhamma Piṭaka): "Knowledge about aging and death is the analytical knowledge of meaning; knowledge about the origin of aging and death is the analytical knowledge of phenomena ... Knowledge about formations is the analytical knowledge of meaning; knowledge about the origin of formations is the analytical knowledge of phenomena."
5. *Attano pana sabhāvaṁ dhārentī ti dhammā.* Dhs.A.39. Despite this definition, the commentries allow to *dhamma* a wider range of meaning than to *sabhāva*. Thus there are *dhammā* which do not support a *sabhāva*, namely, certain conceptual entities and the

attainment of cessation. See the note on the two terms by Ñāṇamoli, Vism., VIII, n.68.

6. See S.XII,11, 23, 27, 66, 69.
7. See S.XII,65; ii,104-5.
8. The distinction is explicitly drawn, with full definitions, in the *Vibhaṅga* (p.137). It does not seem to be stated as such in the suttas, but may have been based on such passages as the following: "If, Ānanda, there were no kamma ripening in the sense-sphere realm, would sense-sphere existence be discerned"? – "Certainly not, venerable sir" (A.III,76; i,223). The *Paṭisambhidāmagga*, too, treats *bhava*, in the context of dependent arising, as identifiable with volition, thus as kamma (Pṭs.i,52).
9. See Appendix for a treatment of this link by way of the *Paṭṭhāna* system of conditions (pp.119-20).
10. For a fuller discussion of the connection between craving and views, see Bodhi, *Net of Views*, pp. 35-36.
11. The Mahānidāna Sutta is not the only discourse of the Buddha which applies dependent arising to the analysis of societal problems. Some other suttas which investigate the chain of conditions underlying social disorder are the Sakkapañha Sutta (D.21), the Mahādukkhakkhandha Sutta (M.13), and the Kalahavivāda Sutta (Sn.IV.11). Despite minor differences in formulation, the conclusions reached are the same.
12. Vism. XVII,187. According to commentarial etymology, the mental factors are called *nāma* because of their bending (*namana*) towards the object in the act of apprehending it. The commentaries also incorporate consciousness into *nāma* on the ground that it too cognizes by bending towards the object. Though *nāma* literally means "name," to use that as a rendering in the present context would be misleading. However, when the mental body is said to be necessary for "designation-contact," this shows that a connection between the original sense of "name" and the doctrinal sense of "mentality" still remains in view.
13. To forestall a misunderstanding which might arise over the ensuing discussion, it should be pointed out here that mind-consciousness is not exclusively introspective, concerned solely with abstract ideas, images, and judgements. Besides arising through the mind-door with purely ideational objects, it can also arise through the

physical sense doors taking the five sense data as objects. All conceptual operations, including the designation and evaluation of sense experience, are the work of mind-consciousness. The five kinds of sense consciousness have the sole function of apprehending their respective sense objects, which they then make available to mind-consciousness for categorization and comprehension. "These five faculties—the faculties of eye, ear, nose, tongue, and body—have different domains, different objects, and do not experience each others' objective domains. The mind is the resort of these five faculties, and mind experiences their objective domains" (M.43; i,295).

14. It should be noted that although there can be no designation-contact *in the material body* without both mentality and materiality, there can be designation-contact in the mental body alone, apart from materiality, namely, in the four immaterial planes of existence. However, the converse does not hold. Since contact is a factor of the mental body there can be no contact of either kind in a bare material body devoid of mentality.

15. The image of a vortex is suggested by Bhikkhu Ñāṇananda, *The Magic of the Mind* (BPS, 1974), pp. 25ff.

16. From the variety of formulated views of self, as will be seen below, it is clear that in principle anything in the personality can be identified as self. But for the spiritually sensitive worldling, consciousness is the prime candidate, as the Buddha indicates: "Bhikkhus, the uninstructed worldling can become disenchanted with this body; he can become dispassionate towards it and liberated from it.... But that which is called mind, mentation, and consciousness, with that he cannot become disenchanted; he cannot become dispassionate towards it and liberated from it. For what reason? Because for a long time, bhikkhus, the uninstructed worldling has been attached to this, has appropriated it, and has misapprehended it thus: 'This is mine, this I am, this is my self.' " (S.XII,61; ii,94). The fourth partial-eternalist view of the Brahmajāla Sutta (D.1; i,21), too, regards the five physical faculties as an impermanent self, "mind, mentation, and consciousness" (*citta, mano, viññāṇa*) as a permanent and changeless self which "will remain the same just like eternity itself" (see *Net of Views*, pp. 72-73).

17. A sutta in the Saṁyutta Nikāya (S.XXII,62; iii,71-73) confirms this identification. It speaks of three "pathways for language, designation, and description": the five aggregates which have ceased

constitute the pathway for the designation "was" (*ahosi*); those aggregates which have not yet arisen constitute the pathway for the designation "will be" (*bhavissati*); and those which have presently arisen constitute the pathway for the designation "is" (*atthi*). As the five aggregates include all phenomena whether internal or external, mentality-materiality here must be intended in the comprehensive sense, as including the outer sense bases as well.

18. The Cūḷavedalla Sutta (M.44; i,301) expresses the same idea thus: "Having previously applied thought and sustained thought, afterwards one breaks out into speech. Therefore applied thought and sustained thought are verbal formations."

19. In later scholastic terminology the contrast is between *parinipphannā dhammā* and *parikappitā dhammā*.

20. The phrase "in principle" is added because in actuality there is a tendency for certain of the basic views to combine with one of the temporal views more readily than with the other. Thus a description of self as limited and material will tend to the annihilationist mode, a description of self as infinite and immaterial will tend to the eternalist mode.

21. If the Buddha's earlier words about the pathway for description are seen as anticipating his exposition of "descriptions of self," perhaps it would not be going too far to see the words about the pathway for designation as relating in a similar way to "considerations of self." The designations would be the thoughts "this I am" and "this is my self" that consummate these considerations. The middle term "language" could then be taken to signify the outward verbal expression of both the designations and the descriptions, which in themselves need not be so expressed. These correlations, however, are conjectural.

22. In making this specification, the commentary assumes that every conception of selfhood implies a positive identification of self with one or another of the aggregates. However, if the alternatives laid out by the Buddha are intended to mirror ordinary thought patterns, insistence on such definiteness may go too far. In ordinary thought (and even in reflection) self may be given an identity simply by being set in relationship to the aggregates, without necessarily being equated with them either individually or collectively. The crucial point is this: that any attempt to identify self must

Kitagiri Sutta

refer it to the aggregates, and this, as we shall see, sets the stage for the demolition of the identification.

23. Cf. the Upanishadic conception of the self as pure bliss (*ānanda*).
24. The argument is stated more fully in the Chachakka Sutta: "If anyone should say, 'Feeling is self,' that is not tenable. For an arising and a falling away of feeling are discerned. Since its arising and falling away are discerned, the consequence would follow: 'My self arises and falls away.' Therefore it is not tenable to say, 'Feeling is self.' Thus feeling is non-self" (M.148; iii,283).
25. See M.72, S.XLIV,7, 8.
26. The commentary defines the two types by statements from the *Puggalapaññatti* (of the Abhidhamma Piṭaka). These statements are identical with the passage from the Kīṭāgiri Sutta except that they explain the distinction with reference to the eight emancipations collectively rather than to the immaterial emancipations alone. In specifying the latter the sutta definition is more lucid and less liable to misinterpretation.
27. See Table 2.
28. The commentary points out that consciousness is also present in the base of neither perception nor non-perception, but in such subtle form that the base cannot be classified among the seven stations. In the four immaterial planes there is no materiality, but only consciousness and mentality.
29. *Samudaya, atthaṅgama, assāda, ādīnava, nissaraṇa.*

PART ONE: THE MAHĀNIDĀNA SUTTA

1. The PTS edition is followed here. The Burmese edition adds *aññamañña-paccayatā pavattati*, "(which) occur as conditions for one another." But this phrase seems to have been mistakenly read from the commentarial gloss into the text itself.
2. *Atathaṁ vā pana santaṁ tathattāya upakappessāmi.* This sentence, enigmatic also in the Pali, renders the original as literally as syntactical requirements will allow. Interpretations are given in the Introduction, p. 31, and in the commentarial exegesis.
3. The Burmese edition reads *ayam aham asmi*, "I am this." The PTS edition's *asmi*, "I am," is confirmed by the commentary. Both editions have *ayam aham asmi* as the reading for the following section.

PART TWO: THE COMMENTARIAL EXEGESIS

1. *Vinayapaññatti, bhummantara, paccayākāra, samayantara.* For a fuller explanation, see *Net of Views*, pp. 130ff.
2. The two extremes are existence and non-existence which harden into the extreme views of eternalism and annihilationism.
3. The Pali word *uttāna* means both "shallow" and "clear." The English translation, which must differ to suit the context, loses the full significance of the analogy.
4. See below, pp. 64-67.
5. The Four Noble Truths. Those "who have seen the truths" (*diṭṭhasaccā*) are Buddhas, paccekabuddhas, and noble disciples.
6. *Mallapāsāṇa.* According to Sub. Cy., a stone which can only be lifted by strong wrestlers.
7. *Yojana.* An ancient Indian linear measurement, equivalent to approximately seven miles.
8. *Pubb'ūpanissayasampatti, titthavāsa, sotāpannatā, bahussutabhāva.*
9. Cy. gives a lengthy account of how the Venerable Ānanda formed his original aspiration; only a synopsis of this is presented here.
10. *Yaṁ kiñci samudayadhammaṁ sabbaṁ taṁ nirodhadhammaṁ.* This is the standard formula for the penetration of the Dhamma achieved by a stream-enterer. See D.i,110, etc.
11. *Atthagambhīratā, dhammagambhīratā, desanāgambhīratā, paṭivedhagambhīratā.*
12. For the nine modes of conditionality, see below, pp. 69-70.
13. The four groups (*saṅkhepa*) are: past causes (ignorance and volitional formations); present results (consciousness through feeling); present causes (craving, clinging, and existence); and future results (birth, and aging-and-death). The three connections (*sandhi*) obtain between past causes and present results, present results and present causes, and present causes and future results. See Vism. XVII,289-90.
14. The expression "course of existence" (*pavatti*) signifies every occasion of existence from the moment following rebirth-linking until death.
15. "Association" (*sampayoga*), as a specific conditional relation in the Abhidhamma system, obtains only between co-existent mental

factors, and thus does not apply to the link between mentality and materiality even though these may be mutually dependent and connected by other conditional relations.

16. "One-constituent existence" (*ekavokārabhava*): the plane of non-percipient beings, who consist exclusively of the aggregate of material form. "Four-constituent existence" (*catuvokārabhava*): the immaterial planes, where the four mental aggregates exist without material form. "Five-constituent existence" (*pañcavokārabhava*): the planes of beings constituted by all five aggregates.

17. "Deformation," as a rendering of *ruppana*, attempts to reproduce in English a word-play in the original Pali, which unetymologically derives the noun *rūpa*, "material form" or "materiality," from the passive verb *ruppati*, "to be worn away," hence "to be deformed."

18. *Uppāda, pavatta, nimitta, āyūhana, saṁyoga, paḷibodha, samudaya, hetu, paccaya.* These nine modes, peculiar to the *Paṭisambhidāmagga*, should not be confused with the twenty-four conditional relations of the *Paṭṭhāna*. The former indicate nine aspects from which any conditioning relationship can be viewed and apply *in toto* to every condition in relation to its effect. The latter indicate particular ways in which the conditioning phenomena function as conditions, and only a select number will apply to any given relationship. The next paragraph attempts to explain the meaning of the nine modes. The passage is obscure even in the original and certain liberties in translation had to be taken to bring implicit connections to light.

19. The commentaries divide full understanding (*pariññā*) into three successive stages. In the first, "full understanding of the known" (*ñātapariññā*), mental and material phenomena are delimited by the defining of their particular characteristics and their conditioned origination is ascertained by the discernment of their conditions. In the second, "full understanding by scrutinization" (*tīraṇapariññā*), those same phenomena are surveyed by way of the three general characteristics: impermanence, suffering, and non-self. In the third, "full understanding by abandoning" (*pahānapariññā*), erroneous conceptions are abandoned by the arising of successive insights leading up to the supramundane path. The insight-knowledges proper begin at this third stage, with the first two stages serving as their foundation.

20. "Comprehension" (*abhisamaya*): a technical term for the functions of the noble path, which include the full understanding of the truth

of suffering and the abandoning of craving, the origin of suffering.

21. *Idaṁsaccābhinivesakāyagantha.* Literally, "the bodily knot of the adherence, 'This is true.' "

22. *Paccayānaṁ nidānaṁ kathitaṁ.*

23. In the *Visuddhimagga* these three qualities of conditionality are interpreted somewhat differently (XVII, 6): "Because each particular phenomenon originates through its appropriate conditions, neither more nor less, it is called 'reality' (*tathatā*). Because, once their conditions reach completeness, there is no non-origination of the phenomena due to be produced through them even for a moment, it is called 'undelusiveness' (*avitathatā*). Since no phenomenon arises through the conditions appropriate to some other phenomenon it is called 'invariability' (*anaññathatā*)." Ven Ñāṇamoli's translation has been modified to bring it into accord with the terminology used above.

24. The three kings are the presiding deities of their respective realms in the "heaven of the four great kings." The fourth, Virūpakkha, is the ruler of the *nāgas*, wonder-working dragons inhabiting the remaining realm. Cy.'s explanation of the last three types of beings differs from the usual account. This is advanced by Sub. Cy., which the renderings chosen here follow.

25. See Introduction, p. 11.

26. *Paranimmitavasavattidevā*: the gods inhabiting the highest of the six sense-sphere heavens.

27. See Introduction, p. 12.

28. Three kinds of kamma-existence and three kinds of rebirth-existence, each having as condition the four kinds of clinging.

29. "Manifestation" (*pariyuṭṭhāna*): a technical term signifying a defilement which has risen up from the stage of underlying tendency to appear in the form of unwholesome thoughts and emotions.

30. *Ñāṇa, taṇhā, diṭṭhi, vitakka.*

31. *Osaraṇasamosaraṇa, sahajātasamosaraṇa, paccayasamosaraṇa.*

32. See Vism. XVII,221.

33. Sensitive matter (*pasādarūpa*), according to the Abhidhamma, is the sensorily receptive matter of the eye, ear, nose, tongue, and body, which enables them to function as bases of cognition. See

Bhikkhu Bodhi, *A Comprehensive Manual of Abhidhamma* (Kandy: BPS, 1993), pp. 238-39.

34. For a description of the modes of occurrence of consciousness referred to here and in the following paragraph, see Vism. XIV, 111-24; *A Comprehensive Manual of Abhidhamma*, pp. 41; 123-24.

35. These refer respectively to each of the four mental aggregates: feeling, perception, mental formations, and consciousness.

36. *Hadayavatthu.* The Pali commentaries, following ancient Indian tradition, regard the heart as the physical basis of mind-consciousness. In the canonical Abhidhamma Piṭaka, however, the basis for consciousness is not specified. The *Paṭṭhāna* only says: "that material form by which mind element and mind-consciousness element are supported."

37. See above, II, n.17.

38. *Sappaṭigha*: namely, the five kinds of sensitive matter. Thus impingement-contact is contact occurring through the five physical sense faculties, eye-contact, ear-contact, etc.

39. In the Abhidhamma, mental objects (*dhammārammaṇa*), apprehended exclusively by mind-consciousness and never by the five-fold sense consciousness, are classified as sixfold: mind, mental factors, sensitive matter, subtle matter, concepts, and nibbāna.

40. The thirty material phenomena that originate along with the rebirth-linking consciousness are grouped into three clusters of ten each: the decads of heart-basis, body, and sex. See Vism. XX, 22, *A Comprehensive Manual of Abhidhamma*, pp. 252-55. According to the Abhidhamma, material phenomena are slower to change than mental phenomena; thus during the time an arisen material phenomenon endures, sixteen acts of consciousness arise and perish.

41. The death-consciousness cannot occur during the sequence of consciousness constituting the rebirth-process.

42. This refers to the division of a moment of consciousness into three sub-moments, made more explicit immediately below.

43. Those "still standing" are the material phenomena originating at the duration moment and dissolution moment of the rebirth-linking consciousness.

44. *Viññāṇamayo attā*. This may be an allusion to a Vedantic conception of the self.

45. For an alternative interpretation of this passage, see Introduction, p. 31.

46. The four in each case should be understood by way of the four descriptions of self.

47. In the Abhidhamma teaching, the rebirth-consciousness is divided into four types by way of roots: triple-rooted (endowed with non-greed, non-hatred, and non-delusion), double-rooted (endowed with non-greed and non-hatred), rootless wholesome resultant, and rootless unwholesome resultant. See *A Comprehensive Manual of Abhidhamma*, pp. 210-16.

48. Ordinarily the "beings in the lower realms" (*vinipātikā*) are identified with the denizens of the four planes of misery. But here the term is used to refer to other classes of beings outside the planes of misery.

49. The shift from the singular to the plural is in the text. Apparently, singular "great Brahmā" is the chief of the great Brahmās.

50. The fivefold system of jhāna is obtained by dividing the second jhāna of the fourfold system into two, one without applied thought but with sustained thought (*avitakka-vicāramatta*) and one with neither applied thought nor sustained thought (*avitakka-avicāra*). Meditators with sharp faculties eliminate the two kinds of thought simultaneously and thus reckon jhāna as fourfold; those lacking such skill must eliminate them sequentially and thus reckon jhāna as fivefold. See Vism. IV, 198-202.

51. Chapter X. The causes for rebirth into these stations are the corresponding meditative attainments.

52. *Saṅkhārāvasesasukhumabhāva*. See Vism. X,47-55.

53. For details, see Vism. XX,97-98.

54. "Without contact with the first jhāna" (*paṭhamajjhānaphassena vinā*). This phrase needs careful qualification. It applies only to the dry-insight meditator, and means that he reaches the supramundane path, by which he penetrates the truths, without having previously attained mundane jhāna. But for all meditators the supramundane path includes jhāna, required to fulfil the "right concentration" factor of the noble eightfold path. In the case of the dry-insight meditator, the concentration factor will occur at

the minimal level as the first supramundane jhāna (see Vism. XXI,112). The four functions of penetration are the full understanding of suffering, the abandonment of its origin (craving), the realization of its cessation (nibbāna), and the development of the path. Each supramundane path performs these functions; the last one, the path of arahatship, completes them. See Vism. XXII, 92-97.

55. Since all the mental functions stop in the attainment of cessation, there can be no "delight in the object."

56. This discussion seems to imply that the four jhānas as such are not emancipations, but become emancipations only by "distinguished development" (*bhāvanāvisesa*).

57. The translation employs two phrases here because the one phrase of the Pali, *dvīhi bhāgehi vimutto*, can be read both as instrumental and as ablative. From the immediately following explanation in the commentary, it is clear that the meanings implied by both readings are intended: that *through which* he is liberated and that *from which* he is liberated.

58. The phrase "some say" (*keci*) is used in the commentarial literature to introduce an opinion rejected by the commentator and the tradition he accepts. The Uttaravihāra, or "Northern Monastery," is the Abhayagiri Vihāra, the heterodox rival of the Mahāvihāra, the centre of strict orthodoxy to whose tradition the Venerables Buddhaghosa and Dhammapāla belonged. The *Sārasamāsa*, "Compendium of the Essence," seems to have been an exegetical work of the Uttaravihāra, possibly their own commentary to the Dīgha Nikāya. For a discussion, see Lily De Silva's Introduction to her PTS edition of the Dīgha Ṭīkā, pp. lix-lxiii.

59. Because the coloured kasiṇas used to achieve the fine-material-sphere jhānas are originally sense objects.

A PALI-ENGLISH GLOSSARY

This glossary includes only the more important doctrinal terms appearing in the Mahānidāna Sutta, its commentary and subcommentary, and in the Introduction, Appendix, and annotations. Only those meanings of a term are given which are intended by its use in this work. Other meanings it may have elsewhere, as well as non-technical uses, are not cited.

akusala—unwholesome
ajjhosāna—attachment
attā—self
attha—(i) meaning; (ii) purpose
atthaṅgama—passing away
adukkhamasukha—neither painful nor pleasant
adhivacana—designation
anaññatha—invariable
anattā—non-self
ananta—infinite
anāgāmī—non-returner
anicca—impermanent
anudiṭṭhi—settled view
anupassanā—contemplation
anubodha—understanding
anubhavana—experiencing
anuloma—forward order
anusaya—underlying tendency
anuseti—to underlie
apāya—plane of misery
appavatti—non-occurrence
abyāpāra—absence of an agent
abhiññā—direct knowledge
abhinandati—to seek enjoyment
abhinibbatti—generation
abhinivesa—(i) adherence; (ii) interpretation
abhisaṅkharaṇa—volitionally forming
arahat—(untranslated) a fully liberated one
ariya—noble, a noble one
arūpa—immaterial
avacara—sphere
avatthā—stage
avabhāsa—appearance
avijjā—ignorance
avitatha—(i) undelusive; (ii) not thus
asañña—non-percipient
asura—titan
assāda—satisfaction
ahaṅkāra—ego-conception
ahetuka—rootless
ākāra—quality, mode
ākāsa—space
ākiñcañña—nothingness
ādīnava—unsatisfactoriness
āyatana—(i) sense base; (ii) base
āyūhana—accumulating, accumulation
ārakkha—safeguarding
ārammaṇa—object

āruppa—immaterial state
āvajjana—adverting (consciousness)
āvāsa—abode (of beings)
āsava—canker
āhāra—nutriment
itthatta—this (present) state of being
idappaccayatā—specific conditionality
indriya—faculty
uccheda—annihilation(ism)
uttāna—clear, shallow
uddesa—indicator
upakappeti—to convert (prepare for, cause to acquire)
upanissaya—decisive support
upapajjati—to re-arise
upādāna—clinging
upekkhā—equanimity
uppattibhava—rebirth-existence
uppāda—arising
ubhatobhāgavimutta—liberated in both ways
ekatta—identity, identical
okkanti—conception
okkamati—to descend
kathā—explanation, talk
kappa—aeon
kamma—action; also untranslated
kammabhava—kamma-existence
kalāpa—cluster
kasiṇa—(untranslated) a device for developing concentration
kāma—(i) sense sphere; (ii) sensual, sense pleasures
kāya—body
kāraṇa—reason, cause
kicca—function
kiriya—functional (class of consciousness)
kilesa—defilement
kusala—wholesome
khaṇa—moment
khandha—aggregate
khaya—destruction
gati—destination
gandhabba—celestial
gambhīra—deep
citta—mind, consciousness
cuti—death, passing away
cetasika—mental factor
cetovimutti—liberation of mind
chanda—desire
jarā—aging
jāti—birth
jhāna—(untranslated) meditative absorption
ñāṇa—knowledge
ñāta—known
ṭhiti—(i) station (for consciousness); (ii) structuring factor; (iii) duration
takkika—rationalist
taṇhā—craving
tatha—thus, real
tathāgata—(untranslated) perfect one
tadārammaṇa—registration (consciousness)
tiracchānayoni—animal realm
tīraṇa—scrutinization
diṭṭhi—view
diṭṭhigatika—theorist
dukkha—suffering, pain, painful
duggati—unfortunate destination
deva—god
desanā—teaching

dhamma—(i) (untranslated) the teaching of the Buddha; (ii) phenomenon; (iii) mental object; (iv) subject to (as suffix)

dhātu—element

nānatta—diversity; diverse

nāma—(i) mentality; (ii) name

nāmarūpa—mentality-materiality

nidāna—source, causation

nimitta—sign

niraya—hell

nirutti—language

nirodha—cessation

nivāsa—abode

nissaraṇa—escape

paccakkha—direct cognition

paccatta—personally

paccaya—condition

paccayākāra—principle of conditionality

paccay'uppanna—conditionally arisen

paccavekkhaṇā—reviewing (knowledge)

paccekabuddha—(untranslated) one privately enlightened

pajānāti—to understand

paññatti—description

paññā—wisdom

paññāpeti—to describe

paññāyati—to be discerned

paññāvimutta—liberated by wisdom

paññāvimutti—liberation by wisdom

paṭicca—in dependence upon

paṭiccasamuppanna—dependently arisen

paṭiccasamuppāda—dependent arising

paṭigha—(i) impingement; (ii) aversion

paṭibhāga—counterpart (sign)

paṭiloma—reverse order

paṭivedha—penetration

paṭisaṁvedana—experience

paṭisandhi—rebirth-linking

patiṭṭha—gained a footing

patha—pathway

paramattha—ultimate sense

parāmāsa—misapprehension

parikappanā—mental construction

pariggaha—(i) possessiveness; (ii) discernment (of conditions)

pariccheda—delimitation

pariññā—full understanding

paritta—limited

parinibbāna—extinguishing

pariyesanā—pursuit

pavatti—(i) occurrence; (ii) course of existence; (iii) application

paveṇī—current (of material phenomena)

pasādarūpa—sensitive matter

pahāna—abandoning, abandonment

pāramī—perfection

puggala—individual

puñña—merit

peta—afflicted spirit

phala—fruit, effect

phassa—contact

bahiddhā—external

bahussuta—highly learned

bhaṅga—dissolution

bhava—existence

bhavaṅga—life-continuum

bhāva—nature, state

bhāvanā—development

bhūta—(i) come to be, become; (ii) being; (iii) material element; (iv) demon

bheda—breakup, division

magga—path

macchariya—stinginess

manasikāra—attention

mano—mind, mentation

mamaṅkāra—conception of "mine"

maraṇa—death

māna—conceit

mūla—root

yakkha—spirit

yoni—mode of origin

rāga—lust, desire

rūpa—(i) material form, material; (ii) fine-material (sphere); (iii) visible form

lakkhaṇa—characteristic

lābha—gain

liṅga—trait

lokiya—mundane

lobha—greed

vacana—statement

vaṭṭa—round (of existence)

vatthu—basis

vaya—falling away; fall

vāda—doctrine

vikkhambhana—suppression

vicāra—sustained thought

viññāṇa—consciousness

vitakka—thought, applied thought

vinaya—(i) (untranslated) monastic discipline; (ii) removal

vinicchaya—decision, decision-making

vinipāta—lower realm

vipariṇāma—change

vipassanā—insight

vipāka—result, resultant (of kamma)

vibhava—non-existence

vimutta—liberated

vimutti—liberation

vimokkha—emancipation

virāga—fading out

vivaṭṭa—ending of the round

visaya—domain

visesa—distinct, distinctive, distinguished, particular, distinction

vedanā—feeling

vedayita—what is felt, feeling

vokkamati—to expire

vokāra—constituent

vohāra—expression

saṁyojana—fetter

saṁsāra—(untranslated) the cycle of rebirths

sakadāgāmī—once-returner

sakkāyadiṭṭhi—personality view

saṅkhata—conditioned

saṅkhāra—(i) volitional formation (ii) mental formation

saṅkhepa—group

sacca—truth

sacchikaroti—to realize

saññā—perception

satipaṭṭhāna—foundation of mindfulness

santati—continuity

santāna—continuum

santīraṇa—investigation (consciousness)

sandhi—connection

sappaṭigha—impingent

sabbaññutā—omniscience

sabhāva—intrinsic nature
samatha—serenity
samanupassati—to consider
samaya—(i) occasion; (ii) tenet
samāpatti—(meditative) attainment
samucchati—to take shape
samuccheda—eradication
samudaya—origin, origination
samudāgata—sustained, produced
samudācāra—obsession
samosaraṇa—convergence
sampaṭicchanna—reception (consciousness)
sambhava—origination
sambhūta—originated
sammasana—exploration (knowledge)
sarasalakkhaṇa—essential characteristic
sassata—eternal(ism)
sahajāta—conascence
sāvaka—disciple
sīlabbata—precepts and observances
sukha—happiness, pleasure, pleasant
subha—beautiful, beauty
sotāpatti—stream-entry
sotāpanna—stream-enterer
hadayavatthu—heart-basis
hetu—cause, root-cause

INDEX

E

F

G

H

I

J

K

L

M

material body (*rūpakāya*), 16-17, 35, 50, 80-82, 106, 123 n.14
Mental formations (*saṅkhārā*), 80, 81
Mentality (*nāma*), 15, 16, 67, 83, 87, 117, 118; mental body (*nāmakāya*), 16, 17, 23, 35, 50, 80-82, 106, 122 n.12, 123 n.14
Mentality-materiality (*nāma-rūpa*), 15-17, 18-22, 25, 46, 50-51, 65-66, 67, 82-90, 117-19
Mindfulness, foundations of (*satipaṭṭhāna*), 37, 97

N

Neither perception nor non-perception, base of (*n'eva saññānāsaññāyatana*), 56, 57, 102
Nibbāna, 97, 107
Non-percipient beings (*asaññasattā*), 56, 57, 87, 101, 102
Non-returner (*anāgāmī*), 68
Nothingness, base of (*ākiñcaññāyatana*), 56, 57
Non-self (*anattā*), 97

O

Once-returner (*sakadāgāmī*), 68
Origin (*samudaya*), 75, 102

P

Paccekabuddha, 61, 68, 69, 71
Padumuttara, Buddha, 63
Passing away (*atthaṅgama*), 102
Path (*magga*), 71, 98, 106, 116, 127, 130-31
Pathways (*patha*), 22-28, 31, 38, 51, 55, 89-90, 97-98
Penetration (*paṭivedha*), 7, 65-66, 67, 69, 70, 71, 103
Perception (*saññā*), 16, 55, 80, 98-102
Perfections (*pāramī*), 68
Personality view (*sakkāyadiṭṭhi*), 33-34, 92-93
Plane of misery (*apāya*), 72, 100
Possessiveness (*pariggaha*), 48-49, 78
Pure abodes, 101
Pursuit (*pariyesanā*), 48, 49-50, 78

R

Rāhu, 62
Reality (*tathatā*), 74-75, 128 n.23
Rebirth-linking (*paṭisandhi*), 18-19, 65, 66, 84-89, 98, 100, 101, 117-18
Resultant (*vipāka*), 74, 77, 79, 83, 87, 115, 117-18
Round of existence (*vaṭṭa*), 3-5, 8, 22, 39, 51, 55, 90, 95-96, 98

S

Safeguarding (*ārakkha*), 48, 78
Saṁsāra, 8, 33-34, 39, 45, 72-73, 89, 90. *See also*: round of existence
Sārasamāsa, 107, 131 n.58
Satisfaction (*assāda*), 56, 102
Self (*attā*), 19-20, 23-26, 66, 67, 89, 123 n.16. *See also*: considerations of self, descriptions of self, settled view (of self)
Sense bases, six (*saḷāyatana*), 14-15, 24, 66, 67, 73-74
Sensitive matter (*pasādarūpa*), 128 n.33, 129 n.38
Serenity (*samatha*), 39, 40, 98, 103
Settled view (of self) (*anudiṭṭhi*), 31-32, 52-53, 91
Specific conditionality (*idappaccayatā*), 8-11, 45-46, 73
Spirits (*yakkhā*), 46, 75, 99
Stations for consciousness, seven (*viññāṇaṭṭhiti*), 39, 55-56, 98-102
Stinginess (*macchariya*), 48-49, 78
Stream-enterer (*sotāpanna*), 63, 68, 100
Suffering (*dukkha*), 2-3, 8, 12, 38, 46, 51
Supaṇṇa bird, 62

T

Tathāgata, 2, 37-38, 55, 97

U

V

W

Of related interest

By the same translator, Bhikkhu Bodhi

The Discourse on The All-Embracing Net of Views

The Brahmajāla Sutta and Its Commentaries

The *Brahmajāla*, one of the Buddha's most important discourses, weaves a net of sixty-two cases capturing all the speculative views on the self and the world. The massive commentary and subcommentary allow for a close in-depth study of the work.

350 pp., hardback BP 209H

The Discourse on The Fruits of Recluseship

The Sāmaññaphala Sutta and Its Commentaries

In reply to a question on the fruits of the monk's life, the Buddha traces the entire progress of the disciple from the first step of the path to its culmination in the attainment of Nibbāna.

200 pp. BP 212S

The Discourse on The Root of Existence

The Mūlapariyāya Sutta and Its Commentaries

This profound and difficult discourse of the Buddha aims at exposing and eliminating the concept of the ego at its most fundamental level. The commentary offers a detailed explanation of the sutta while a long introduction provides a detailed guide to the text's meaning and its implications for philosophy and psychology.

90 pp. BP 210S

THE BUDDHIST PUBLICATION SOCIETY

The BPS is an approved charity dedicated to making known the Teaching of the Buddha, which has a vital message for people of all creeds. Founded in 1958, the BPS has published a wide variety of books and booklets covering a great range of topics. Its publications include accurate annotated translations of the Buddha's discourses, standard reference works, as well as original contemporary expositions of Buddhist thought and practice. These works present Buddhism as it truly is—a dynamic force which has influenced receptive minds for the past 2500 years and is still as relevant today as it was when it first arose. A full list of our publications will be sent upon request. Write to:

The Hony. Secretary
BUDDHIST PUBLICATION SOCIETY
P.O. Box 61
54, Sangharaja Mawatha
Kandy • Sri Lanka
E–mail: bps@ids.lk
Website: http: //www.lanka.com/dhamma